FORGIVING BULLIES IN YOUR FAMILY

21 Day Journal To Transform Pain Into Compassion And Rebuild Relationships With Strength and Grace

Blending Our Love, Maryland

Copyright © 2023 by Tuniscia Okeke

Published 2023

Library of Congress Cataloging-in-Publication Data

ISBN: 978-1-962748-32-2 (Print)

ISBN:978-1-962748-33-9 (eBook)

Printed in the United States of America

FORGIVING BULLIES IN YOUR FAMILY

21 Day Journal To Transform Pain Into Compassion And Rebuild Relationships With Strength and Grace

TUNISCIA OKEKE

BLENDING OUR LOVE, INC.

DEDICATION

I found my voice.

Table of Contents

Paying It Forward

I'm sharing this message as the author of this 21-day journal on forgiveness, not just with words on these pages but with a story that has shaped my life's purpose. As I embark on this journey with you, I want to share the deeply personal and transformative experiences that led me to write, edit, and self-publish 35 books on forgiveness in less than a year.

My forgiveness journey began when I was 24, a pivotal age when life often feels like an open book, brimming with hope and dreams. Then, my mother called me on a seemingly ordinary Monday morning, and with those words, she unraveled the narrative of my life. She revealed that the man I had believed to be my father for all those years was, in fact, not my biological father.

The weight of that revelation was crushing. It was as if the ground beneath me had shifted, leaving me unsteady and disoriented. But what shook me to my core was not the revelation itself but the sudden rupture of trust in my mother—the person I had always looked up to as a paragon of love, trustworthiness, and honesty.

In the wake of this revelation, I spiraled into a bottomless pit of resentment, anger, and pain. I grappled with a profound sense of betrayal and felt adrift in a sea of unanswered questions. It was a turbulent period in my life, and for 17 long years, I carried the heavy burden of unforgiveness.

Then, something remarkable happened that would alter the course of my life forever. I noticed a pattern in my relationship with my children. They treated me with a lack of respect and love, leaving me bewildered and hurt. In desperation, I turned to prayer one day, seeking answers from a higher source.

God's voice whispered into my heart in that sacred space of prayer and introspection, revealing a profound truth: "I taught them how to love me by the way I loved my mother."

Those words struck me like lightning, piercing through the fog of my confusion. It was an awakening—a profound realization that, in my quest for revenge against my mother, I had unwittingly passed on the energy of resentment to my children. I had normalized my hurtful behaviors as the way we should treat our mothers.

On my 40th birthday, I consciously confronted my soul's deepest and darkest corners. I embarked on a journey of healing, self-forgiveness, and forgiveness of my mother. My primary motivation was to restore my relationship with my children and teach them how to pass on healing, love, and forgiveness to their children.

That six-year odyssey of healing was transformative beyond measure. It led me to write 35 journals, each addressing a facet of forgiveness and healing I encountered on my journey. These journals became my way of reaching out to others grappling with their forgiveness journeys.

Today, I extend a heartfelt invitation to you to embark on this 21-day journey with me. Just as my healing journey began with a single journal, this journal can be your compass for forgiveness, healing, and growth.

I send you loving energy as you navigate through the complexities of your forgiveness journey, and I hope these pages serve as a guiding light toward wholeness and inner peace.

With love and compassion,

Tuniscia O

FOREWARD

A Heartfelt Letter from the Author

Dear Brave Souls,

As you embark on this profound 21-day journey of "Forgiving The Bullies In Your Family," my heart swells with admiration and compassion for each of you. Your decision to undertake this transformative path toward healing and forgiveness is a testament to your strength and resilience.

I want you to know that you are not alone on this journey. We walk this path together as a community of individuals who have experienced the pain caused by those who were supposed to protect and love us. Your commitment to facing these painful experiences head-on is an act of courage that will not go unnoticed.

Over the next 21 days, we will explore the intricate layers of forgiveness, healing, and resilience. We will delve into the power of empathy, self-compassion, and setting healthy boundaries. We will share our stories, embracing vulnerability as our guiding light. Together, we will learn that forgiveness is not about condoning hurtful actions but liberating ourselves from anger and resentment.

I want you to understand that healing is not linear. There may be moments when you stumble when the pain resurfaces, but please remember that it's all part of the process. Every step forward, regardless of its size, is a victory. Each day you choose forgiveness, you choose to free yourself from the burden of the past.

As we embark on this journey, I encourage you to carry the lessons and insights you gain into your daily life. Let compassion guide your interactions, and may the strength you discover within yourself become a beacon of hope for others who may be walking a similar path.

Thank you for allowing me to be a part of your journey. Your trust and unwavering dedication to healing and forgiveness inspire me. Together, we will show that it is possible to transform pain into compassion and rebuild relationships with strength and grace.

With heartfelt gratitude and warm wishes for your continued growth and healing,

Tuniscia O

The Cycle of Generational Behavior

Family, often considered a sanctuary of love and support, family can sometimes become the breeding ground for bullying behavior. The notion of family members bullying each other, especially when older individuals prey on younger, weaker ones, is a perplexing and profoundly concerning issue. This essay delves into the intricate web of reasons behind family bullying, the dynamics that enable it, and the ripple effects it can have beyond the family unit.

Learned Behavior

Family bullying often begins as a learned behavior, with parents or older family members unwittingly passing down the patterns of behavior they may have endured during their youth. This transference of bullying behavior is often rooted in their experiences of victimization. They may view it as a means of discipline or believe that subjecting the younger generation to teasing or taunting will toughen them up.

This process of learned behavior can extend beyond parents and involve other family members such as grandparents or aunts. It often starts under the guise of harmless "teasing," but it may gradually cross the line into more harmful and hurtful territory as it continues.

Recognizing this learned behavior as a root cause is crucial in addressing family bullying. It underscores the importance of breaking the cycle and fostering healthier communication and interaction within the family. By understanding the origins of this behavior, individuals can work towards healing and creating a more nurturing family environment.

Lack of Awareness

Lack of awareness plays a significant role in the perpetuation of family bullying. Often, family members engaging in bullying may not even realize that their actions constitute bullying. They might view their conduct as usual, justified, or even as a form of tough love, making breaking the cycle challenging.

This lack of awareness often stems from the fact that family bullying may have also been a part of their upbringing. Growing up in an environment where such behavior is normalized can lead individuals to repeat it without recognizing its harmful effects.

Furthermore, the cycle of family bullying can be deeply ingrained in the family's dynamics, and over time, it may come to be accepted as the norm. Younger family members who witness these behaviors may believe that this is how families interact, perpetuating the cycle into future generations.

Breaking the cycle of family bullying requires a heightened awareness of what constitutes bullying behavior and a willingness to acknowledge and address it. Shining a light on these harmful dynamics and encouraging open conversations within the family, individuals can begin to challenge and change these ingrained patterns, fostering a healthier family environment for present and future generations.

Factors Contributing to Family Bullying

Stress and Frustration

Stress and frustration are potent catalysts for family bullying, intensifying the tensions that may already exist within the household. External stressors such as financial difficulties, job pressures, or personal issues can create a volatile atmosphere, increasing the likelihood of emotional outbursts and bullying behavior.

In times of high stress, family members may find it challenging to cope with their emotions healthily. This can lead to harmful coping mechanisms, including lashing out at others, particularly within the family unit where emotions are often laid bare.

The frustration stemming from these external stressors can act as a trigger, causing family members to release their pent-up emotions through bullying behavior. Unfortunately, this form of emotional release can create a vicious cycle, as it fails to address the underlying stressors and adds to the family's emotional turmoil.

Recognizing the impact of stress and frustration on family dynamics is crucial for breaking the cycle of bullying. Finding healthier ways to cope with external pressures, fostering open communication, and seeking support can help family members navigate difficult times without resorting to harmful behavior. Families can create a more harmonious and supportive environment by addressing the root causes of stress and frustration and learning more constructive ways to cope.

Power Dynamics

Power dynamics play a significant role in family bullying, with older family members often exploiting their positions of authority. This misuse of power allows them to dominate and control younger, more vulnerable members, creating a breeding ground for bullying behavior.

Within a family, there is typically an established hierarchy that often revolves around age and seniority. Older family members may perceive themselves as decision-makers or authority figures, leading them to assert dominance over younger members. This power imbalance can be particularly pronounced in multigenerational households, where grandparents, parents, and children coexist.

Bullying behaviors may manifest as attempts to exert control, belittling, or manipulation, reinforcing the power dynamic. Younger family members may feel helpless and fearful of challenging the authority figures, further perpetuating the cycle of bullying.

Addressing power dynamics within the family is essential to break the cycle of bullying. Encouraging open communication, fostering respect for each family member's individuality, and promoting a collaborative decision-making process help rebalance the power structure. By recognizing the harm caused by exploiting authority and working towards a more equitable family dynamic, families can create a safer and healthier environment for all members.

Unresolved Conflicts

Unresolved conflicts within a family can act as a potent fuel for bullying behaviors. These lingering disputes or unresolved issues create an atmosphere of tension and frustration that may find an outlet in bullying as family members struggle to cope with their unresolved emotions.

When family members harbor unaddressed conflicts, these emotions can fester over time, leading to heightened resentment and anger. In such an environment, it becomes easier for individuals to resort to bullying tactics to vent their frustration or regain control. This might manifest as verbal abuse, emotional manipulation, or physical intimidation.

The lack of resolution in family conflicts can also lead to a cycle of retribution, where one family member's mistreatment is seen as justified retaliation for past grievances. This cycle can perpetuate the bullying behavior and deepen the rifts within the family.

Open and honest communication is vital to address family bullying stemming from unresolved conflicts. Encouraging family members to express their feelings and concerns, facilitating mediation or counseling, and working together to find resolutions can help diffuse tension and prevent bullying behaviors from taking root. Breaking this cycle requires a commitment to resolving conflicts constructively and nurturing healthier family dynamics.

Projection of Insecurities

The projection of insecurities is a psychological mechanism that can contribute to family bullying. Sometimes, family members may unconsciously project their insecurities onto others, especially younger relatives, to deflect attention from their perceived flaws and inadequacies.

When individuals grapple with feelings of self-doubt, low self-esteem, or unresolved issues from their past, they may seek to externalize these negative emotions. This externalization often takes the form of belittling, criticizing, or demeaning younger or more vulnerable family members.

By projecting their insecurities onto others, these individuals attempt to shift the focus away from their vulnerabilities and onto someone else. This can manifest as verbal abuse, emotional manipulation, or attempts to control and dominate younger family members. Sometimes, the bully may derive a false sense of superiority by making others feel inferior.

Recognizing this dynamic within a family is crucial for addressing and healing the issue of family bullying. Encouraging open and empathetic communication, providing emotional support, and helping family members confront their insecurities can be critical steps in breaking the cycle of bullying behavior. By addressing the root causes of projection, families can work toward healthier and more empathetic relationships.

Fear of Vulnerability

Fear of vulnerability can be a driving force behind family bullying. Some individuals resort to bullying behavior within their family dynamics to shield themselves from feelings of vulnerability or insecurity. This behavior often stems from a misguided belief that they can protect themselves from perceived threats or emotional exposure by asserting dominance and control.

In this context, bullying becomes a defense mechanism to deflect attention from their insecurities and vulnerabilities. These individuals may fear being seen as weak or imperfect, so they adopt a facade of strength and authority through bullying tactics. They erroneously equate dominance with safety.

This fear of vulnerability can create a toxic cycle within a family, as younger or more vulnerable members may internalize the belief that they must conform to the bully's demands to avoid conflict or criticism. It perpetuates a culture of silence and submission, making it challenging to break free from the cycle of family bullying.

Addressing this aspect of family bullying involves fostering a safe and open environment where vulnerability is not seen as a weakness but as an essential element of human connection and growth. Encouraging family members to express their emotions and fears without judgment can be crucial in dismantling the fear of vulnerability and promoting healthier relationships within the family unit.

Bullying Starts At Home

Modeling Behavior

Modeling behavior is a significant factor in understanding why family members sometimes bully. Children, in particular, are highly impressionable and tend to mimic the behaviors they witness at home. When they grow up in an environment where bullying is normalized or accepted, they are likelier to adopt these behaviors and carry them into their interactions with peers at school or in other social settings.

Children look to their parents and older family members as role models for navigating the world. If they witness bullying or aggressive behavior within the family, they may perceive it as an acceptable means of asserting themselves or resolving conflicts. This modeling of behavior can create a vicious cycle where the same patterns of bullying are perpetuated from one generation to the next.

To break this cycle, parents and caregivers must be mindful of their behavior and its impact on their children. Creating a safe and nurturing home environment that promotes healthy communication and conflict resolution can help children learn more positive ways of interacting with others. By modeling empathy, kindness, and respect, adults can guide their children toward healthier relationships and reduce the likelihood of them perpetuating bullying behaviors outside the family.

Impact On Relationships

The impact of bullying within the family goes beyond the immediate family dynamics; it can significantly affect an individual's ability to form and maintain positive relationships outside the home. This is particularly true for children who grow up in an environment where bullying is prevalent.

First and foremost, bullying erodes trust. When family members engage in hurtful or abusive behaviors, it creates an atmosphere of distrust and insecurity. Children who experience bullying within the family may struggle to trust others, including peers, teachers, and friends. This lack of trust can hinder their ability to build healthy relationships based on mutual respect and openness.

Furthermore, bullying can damage communication skills. Children may not learn effective communication strategies in a family where aggressive or hurtful language is the norm. They may have difficulty expressing themselves, resolving conflicts, or understanding the importance of empathy and active listening in relationships.

These challenges can carry over into adulthood, impacting an individual's personal and professional relationships. Breaking free from the cycle of family bullying and seeking support, such as therapy or counseling, can be essential steps in building and maintaining healthy, trusting relationships outside the family unit.

Awareness And Recognition

Awareness and recognition are foundational steps in breaking the cycle of family bullying. Family members must acknowledge that such harmful behaviors exist within their dynamics and have the potential to cause lasting damage.

Recognizing family bullying requires a willingness to confront uncomfortable truths. Often, family members may minimize or rationalize these behaviors, viewing them as usual or harmless teasing. However, it's essential to understand that even seemingly minor bullying incidents can have significant and long-lasting impacts.

Awareness involves educating oneself about the various forms of bullying, from emotional and verbal abuse to physical aggression. It also means recognizing the family's signs and patterns of bullying, such as repeated hurtful comments, belittling, manipulation, or using power and control.

Once awareness and recognition take hold, family members can start to address the issue. This may involve open and honest conversations, seeking professional help or counseling, and a commitment to changing the family dynamics. Breaking the cycle of family bullying is a challenging but essential endeavor, as it benefits the current generation and prevents the perpetuation of these harmful behaviors into the lives of younger family members.

Open Communication

Open communication is a cornerstone in breaking the cycle of family bullying. It fosters an environment where family members can express themselves honestly, respectfully, and without fear of judgment. This open dialogue is vital in addressing conflicts and challenges within the family dynamics.

Encouraging open communication means creating space for family members to share their thoughts, emotions, and concerns. It involves active listening, empathy, and validation of each person's perspective. By doing so, family members can better understand one another's experiences and work together to find solutions.

In family bullying, open communication allows individuals to voice their grievances, whether they are the perpetrators or victims of such behavior. It allows family members to confront the issue head-on, acknowledge its presence, and commit to positive change.

Moreover, open communication can help family members build stronger bonds and trust. It promotes healthier relationships based on mutual respect and understanding. By fostering a culture of open dialogue, families can transform their dynamics and create an environment where bullying behaviors have no place, paving the way for healing, growth, and healthier relationships.

Seeking Professional Help

Seeking professional help is a crucial step in addressing severe family bullying. Therapists and counselors are trained to provide guidance, support, and interventions that can help families break free from harmful behavior patterns and build healthier relationships.

Therapy offers a safe and confidential space for family members to explore the underlying causes of bullying behavior and its impact on individuals and the family unit. A therapist can help family members gain insight into their actions and emotions, facilitating empathy and understanding among family members.

Additionally, therapists can teach families effective communication skills, conflict resolution techniques, and strategies for setting and respecting boundaries. They can also help individuals address underlying issues such as unresolved conflicts, past traumas, or mental health concerns that may contribute to bullying behavior.

In cases where bullying has had a profound impact on the well-being of family members, therapy can be a source of healing and recovery. It provides a supportive environment for individuals to process their experiences, heal emotional wounds, and develop coping strategies.

Overall, seeking professional help is a proactive and constructive approach to addressing family bullying, promoting positive change, and fostering healthier family dynamics. It signifies a commitment to healing, growth, and the well-being of everyone involved.

Family bullying is a complex issue rooted in a web of generational behavior, psychological factors, and unresolved conflicts. Understanding why family members bully each other and recognizing its negative impact on individuals and relationships is crucial. Breaking this cycle requires awareness, open communication, and a commitment to creating a safe and loving family environment where bullying has no place. Addressing family bullying can ultimately pave the way for healthier, more nurturing relationships both within and outside the family unit.

Breaking The Chains

I n the intricate tapestry of life, few threads are as profoundly influential as the bonds within our family. These connections, woven by shared experiences, blood ties, and history, shape our identities and guide our journeys. But what occurs when these bonds become twisted, tarnished, and agonizing? What happens when the sanctuary of a family turns into a battlefield of emotional abuse and bullying?

This journal, "Forgiving The Bullies In Your Family," is a guiding light for those trapped in the shadows of familial toxicity. It serves as an exploration of the raw, unspoken wounds that linger in the corridors of our past and a roadmap to reclaiming the power to heal, forgive, and embrace a future filled with growth and liberation.

Within the pages of this journal, you will embark on a transformative journey. It is a journey of self-discovery, self-compassion, and self-liberation. It invites you to confront the pain and scars of the past with courage and resilience, recognizing that the power to break free from the chains of family bullying lies within you.

You will delve deep into your experiences, unearthing the buried emotions and unspoken truths that may have haunted you for far too long. Through introspection and reflection, you will uncover the roots of your pain, gaining insight into how family dynamics and past experiences have shaped your present self.

As you navigate this journey, you will encounter exercises and prompts designed to guide you toward forgiveness, healing, and growth. You will learn to set healthy boundaries, release self-blame, and embrace self-compassion. Each step will bring you closer to the light of liberation, allowing you to emerge from the shadows of family toxicity and into a future of empowerment.

So, as you embark on this profound journey of forgiveness and healing, remember that you are not alone. This journal is your companion, your confidant, and your guide. Together, we will navigate the labyrinth of family wounds, and together, we will discover the strength and resilience that reside within you, waiting to be unleashed.

Unmasking The Bullying Within The Family

In the sacred realm of family, where love and support should thrive, a dark underbelly of bullying often exists. This insidious behavior can manifest in various ways, from subtle manipulation to outright verbal and emotional abuse. It's a painful reality that many individuals face within the confines of their own homes.

Unmasking this bullying within the family is the first step toward understanding and healing. By shedding light on the hurtful words, actions, and attitudes that persist behind closed doors, we begin to acknowledge the pain inflicted upon us. It's a painful but necessary validation process, recognizing that we are not alone in our experiences.

During our time together, you will create a safe space to confront the bullying you've endured within your family. It emphasizes the importance of breaking the silence that often shrouds these painful experiences, encouraging open dialogue, and seeking support from others who have faced similar challenges.

Unmasking this family bullying lays the groundwork for healing and transformation. You empower yourself to confront the past, set healthy boundaries, and break free from the cycle of abuse. This journal serves as a beacon of hope, reminding you that you can reclaim your life and build healthier, more nurturing family dynamics. It is an invitation to acknowledge the pain, face it head-on, and ultimately, emerge from the darkness into a brighter, more empowered future.

The Shackles Of The Past

The shackles of the past are weighty and unforgiving, especially when forged within the confines of our own families. With its insidious nature, family bullying leaves an indelible mark on our lives, influencing how we view ourselves and the world around us.

Explore the profound impact of family bullying, shedding light on the scars long after the hurtful words have faded. Delving into how emotional abuse within the family can erode our self-esteem, leaving us with a distorted self-image and a constant sense of inadequacy. The wounds inflicted by family members can shape our relationships, causing us to struggle with trust, intimacy, and vulnerability.

Understanding the deep-seated impact of family bullying is an essential step toward healing. It allows us to recognize how we may have internalized the hurtful messages and beliefs imposed upon us. By unraveling the complex web of emotions and insecurities stemming from these experiences, we gain insight into our behavior, choices, and relationship patterns.

Acknowledging the lasting effects of family bullying doesn't mean surrendering to its grip; it means taking control of our narrative. It empowers us to break free from the chains of the past and embark on a journey of self-discovery and healing. Through self-awareness and self-compassion, we can begin to release the shackles that have held us captive for far too long, forging a path toward a brighter, more empowered future.

Emotional Liberation

The power of forgiveness is a profound journey that ultimately leads to emotional liberation, and it all begins with understanding its true essence. Forgiveness is not a declaration of acceptance for the wrongs inflicted upon us; it is a profound act of self-compassion and empowerment.

In exploring the transformative nature of forgiveness, we unveil its profound impact on our emotional well-being. Unraveling the misconception that forgiving someone equates to excusing their actions is crucial. Instead, forgiveness is a gift we offer ourselves, a potent step toward liberation from resentment and bitterness.

Forgiveness liberates us from our emotional burdens, lightening the weight on our hearts. It enables us to break free from the destructive cycles of anger and hurt, granting us the freedom to heal and rebuild our lives on our terms. Through forgiveness, we open ourselves to the possibility of personal growth and transformation, reclaiming our power to shape our narrative.

As we journey through forgiveness, it becomes evident that self-compassion, understanding, and empathy are essential companions. By embracing forgiveness, we not only unburden ourselves from the weight of the past but also pave the way for a future filled with emotional liberation and healing. It is a profound process that, when fully embraced, empowers us to rewrite our stories and find strength in vulnerability and compassion.

Navigating The Healing Journey

Navigating the healing journey from the wounds inflicted by family bullying is a complex and often non-linear process reminiscent of traversing a labyrinthine maze. Each twist and turn reveals new insights, challenges, and opportunities for growth.

We recognize that healing requires a holistic approach that nourishes the mind and body. Exploring self-care routines, such as mindfulness, meditation, exercise, and creative expression, empowers individuals to mend the broken pieces of their emotional well-being. These practices act as a soothing balm for the wounded soul, offering solace and strength along the healing journey.

The significance of setting healthy boundaries within family dynamics cannot be overstated. Establishing limitations is crucial in protecting one's emotional well-being and preventing further harm.

The healing journey vividly depicts the various signposts along the path. It highlights the importance of self-compassion, self-forgiveness, and self-discovery. Ultimately, this journey is about repairing past wounds and transforming oneself into a stronger, more resilient, and emotionally empowered individual. It is a testament to the human spirit's capacity to heal and emerge from adversity with newfound strength and wisdom.

Reclaiming Your Space And Identity

Reclaiming your space is pivotal on your journey toward healing from family bullying. It recognizes the fundamental importance of establishing healthy boundaries within the family context to safeguard your emotional well-being, redefine your identity, and regain control over your life.

This process begins by emphasizing the significance of boundaries in fostering self-respect and protection. It underscores how setting and maintaining boundaries can shield against further emotional harm.

Moreover, it highlights the impact of boundaries on your sense of identity. Family bullying can gradually erode one's self-esteem and identity over time. By setting and maintaining boundaries, you begin redefining yourself, no longer solely defined by the expectations or treatment of others.

As you progress through this journey, you discover that setting boundaries is not an act of aggression but an act of self-care and self-preservation. It is a means of creating a safe and nurturing space where you can flourish and heal.

Reclaiming your space empowers you to take charge of your emotional well-being, allowing you to regain your sense of self and move on the path to healing and personal growth.

Writing A New Chapter Of Empowerment

Embracing growth marks the transition from healing to thriving in your recovery from family bullying. It underscores that the narrative doesn't culminate with forgiveness and healing but continues into a personal growth and empowerment story.

One of the key messages conveyed is that you can shape your narrative. You are not defined by the scars or the pain inflicted upon you. Instead, you have the power to script a new story, one that celebrates your resilience and transformation.

This step encourages you to step into your authenticity. It prompts you to reflect on your passions, dreams, and values and to envision a future that aligns with them. By doing so, you can create a roadmap for personal growth and empowerment that is uniquely yours.

Embracing growth is the transition from being a survivor to becoming a thriver. It empowers you to envision and create a life that reflects your newfound strength, resilience, and authenticity. By embracing growth, you are not merely healing; you are writing a new story of empowerment in your life's narrative.

Inspiring Change For Generations

Inspiring change underscores the transformative impact of sharing your story and experiences with others. It recognizes that your journey of healing and growth can become a powerful source of inspiration and positive change for generations to come.

This step emphasizes the significance of authenticity in your interactions with others. It encourages you to be open about your experiences with family bullying and your path toward healing and empowerment. Doing so creates a safe space for others to share their stories and seek support.

Consider the ripple effect of breaking the cycle of family bullying. By courageously addressing and healing from the wounds of the past, you not only transform your own life but also contribute to a healthier and more compassionate family culture. This positive change can profoundly impact future generations, sparing them from the pain and trauma they may have endured.

Sharing your light is about nurturing authentic relationships. It highlights the importance of surrounding yourself with individuals who respect your boundaries, support your growth, and share in your journey towards empowerment. Additionally, it encourages you to be a source of support for others who may be struggling with similar experiences.

Remember that your story is not just yours; it has the potential to inspire and catalyze change in others. By sharing your light, you become a beacon of hope for those on their path of healing and transformation. Your willingness to be vulnerable and authentic can create a ripple effect extending far beyond your life, ultimately inspiring change for future generations.

Writing Your New Narrative

Writing your new narrative stands as the guiding principle in our journey of healing and growth beyond the scars of family bullying. While the wounds inflicted by family bullying may have left their mark, they need not dictate the course of your life. You are the sole author of your narrative, endowed with the creative power to determine how your story unfolds from this moment onward. The painful experiences of the past can serve as valuable lessons, catalysts for personal growth, and reservoirs of inner strength.

In this transformative journey, you wield the agency to compose a new narrative imbued with healing, forgiveness, and growth. Your life's tapestry is a complex weave of experiences—trials, and triumphs— that create a unique and intricate design together. Family bullying may have cast shadows on some portions of this tapestry, but it does not define the entirety of your narrative.

As you embark on this journey, embrace the role of an author shaping a fresh narrative. Explore the chapters of your life with a sense of curiosity and self-compassion. Recognize that your past does not dictate your future; it merely informs it. The challenges you've faced, the wounds you've endured, and the resilience you've discovered all contribute to the rich tapestry of your existence.

With each step forward in healing and growth, you craft a narrative that reflects your newfound strength and wisdom. The pain of the past does not bind the pages of your story; they are infused with the potential for transformation and empowerment. As you write your new narrative, may it be a testament to the resilience of the human spirit and the boundless capacity for growth and healing.

Why It's Normalized

Bullying is a pervasive issue that affects people in various settings, including schools, workplaces, and online communities. However, one of the lesser-discussed aspects of bullying is its occurrence within families. It's not uncommon for individuals to experience bullying from family members, but the normalization of such behavior makes this phenomenon particularly complex. This essay delves into why people may normalize being bullied within their families, its profound impact on their relationships, and the importance of breaking this cycle.

Lack of Awareness

A lack of awareness is a significant factor in normalizing family bullying. Many individuals grow up in households where certain behaviors, such as emotional manipulation, belittling, or intimidation, are considered the norm. These behaviors may have been passed down through generations, creating a family culture where bullying is tolerated or accepted.

In such environments, family members may not fully grasp the extent of the harm being done. They might believe that what they are experiencing is just a part of family life or how families interact. This lack of awareness can lead them to downplay or dismiss the emotional and psychological toll that family bullying takes on their well-being.

Additionally, individuals subjected to family bullying from a young age may internalize these behaviors as usual. They may grow up thinking that treating others this way is acceptable, perpetuating the cycle into adulthood and future relationships.

Breaking free from the cycle of family bullying begins with raising awareness about what constitutes healthy and respectful family dynamics. It involves recognizing that bullying behaviors, regardless of origin, are harmful and unacceptable. By acknowledging the issue and seeking support or education, individuals can take the first step toward breaking the cycle and fostering healthier family relationships.

Fear Of Confrontation

Fear of confrontation is a significant barrier to addressing family bullying. Many victims and witnesses of bullying within the family may be hesitant to confront the abusive behavior for several reasons, including:

Fear of Retaliation: Fear of retaliation is a significant barrier to addressing family bullying. Victims worry that confronting the bully may lead to even more aggression or reprisals. This fear often prevents them from challenging the abusive behavior, allowing the cycle of family bullying to persist.

Breaking this cycle requires creating a safe and supportive environment where victims and witnesses feel empowered to speak out against bullying without fear of repercussions. Education and awareness about the harmful effects of bullying and the available resources for support can help individuals overcome this fear and take steps toward ending family bullying.

Strained Relationships: Strained relationships within the family can deter individuals from addressing bullying behavior. Concerns about confronting the bully may further lead to fears of damaging family relationships. The worry of creating estrangement or conflict among family members is often a barrier to addressing family bullying.

To break this cycle, it's essential to emphasize that addressing the issue can lead to healthier, more respectful relationships within the family in the long run, even if initial confrontations are challenging. Education and support can help individuals navigate these concerns and work towards ending family bullying.

Making the Situation Worse: Many victims of family bullying fear that addressing the issue will only worsen it. They may believe that confronting the bully will lead to increased aggression, both emotionally and potentially physically. This fear can be a significant deterrent to seeking help or attempting to break the cycle of family bullying.

It's essential to emphasize that addressing bullying, though initially challenging, is a crucial step toward ending the cycle and promoting healthier family dynamics in the long term. Providing support and resources for individuals facing this fear can empower them to take action against family bullying.

Overcoming the fear of confrontation is essential for breaking the cycle of family bullying. It requires creating a safe environment where victims and witnesses feel supported and empowered to speak out against abusive behavior. Education and awareness about the harmful effects of bullying and the available resources for support can help individuals overcome their fears and take steps toward addressing and ultimately ending family bullying.

Cultural And Societal Norms

Cultural and societal norms can strongly influence the normalization of family bullying. In certain cultures, there may be a strong emphasis on hierarchical family structures where older family members hold more authority, which can be misused to perpetuate bullying behaviors. Similarly, traditional gender roles within some societies may contribute to power imbalances and bullying dynamics.

Furthermore, societal attitudes and perceptions can play a role in normalizing family bullying. Society, as a whole, may sometimes downplay or minimize family bullying, making it challenging for individuals to recognize and address these harmful behaviors. Breaking free from these cultural and societal norms can be a complex process. Still, promoting healthier family dynamics and ending the cycle of family bullying is essential. It requires awareness, education, and a shift in societal attitudes toward recognizing and condemning family bullying as unacceptable.

Impact Of Being Bullied

Overly Aggressive or Isolated Behavior

Normalization of family bullying can manifest in various ways, including overly aggressive or isolated behavior in individuals who have experienced it. Those subjected to bullying within their families may replicate these behaviors in their relationships, becoming overly aggressive as a defense mechanism or a way to assert control.

Conversely, some individuals may withdraw and become isolated, fearing vulnerability and potential harm in their interactions. This isolation can lead to difficulty forming healthy relationships, as they may struggle with trust and intimacy.

Recognizing these behavioral patterns and their roots in family bullying is crucial for individuals seeking to break free from its cycle. Through self-awareness, therapy, and support, they can work towards healthier ways of relating to others, understanding that aggressive or isolated behavior often stems from past trauma and the normalization of bullying within the family context. Healing and breaking the cycle involve acknowledging these patterns and actively working towards healthier, more compassionate relationships.

Fear of Physical Conflict

The normalization of family bullying can instill a deep-seated fear of physical conflict in individuals, making them opposed to any form of confrontation, even when necessary for healthy communication and conflict resolution. This fear can have far-reaching consequences, hindering the development of open and honest relationships.

Individuals who have grown up in an environment where family bullying was normalized often associate conflict with violence or harm. As a result, they may go to great lengths to avoid any situation that might lead to disagreement or confrontation, even in non-abusive settings.

This fear can create barriers to effective communication, as open dialogue and expressing differing opinions become viewed as threatening. Over time, it can suppress one's thoughts and emotions, making it challenging to form meaningful and authentic connections with others.

Breaking free from the fear of physical conflict and its impact on relationships requires self-awareness and a commitment to personal growth. Therapy, support groups, and self-help resources can all be valuable tools in overcoming this fear and learning to navigate healthy conflict in a way that promotes growth and healing.

Fear of Telling the Truth

The fear of telling the truth is a common consequence of growing up in an environment where family bullying is normalized. In such households, honesty may have been discouraged or even met with punishment, causing individuals to associate truth-telling with negative consequences. This fear can profoundly affect their ability to trust and communicate openly in their relationships.

Individuals who have experienced family bullying may become hesitant to share their true thoughts and feelings, even in non-abusive settings. They may worry that being honest will lead to conflict or rejection, as seen in their family dynamics. This fear of truth-telling can hinder the development of authentic and meaningful connections with others.

Breaking free from this fear requires recognizing its origins and working towards building a healthier relationship with honesty. Therapy and support groups provide a safe space for individuals to explore their fears and develop strategies for fostering trust and transparency in their relationships. Over time, they can learn that telling the truth does not have to result in negative consequences and that authentic connections are built on trust and open communication.

Exploring Self-Perpetuated Bullying

Accepting Bullying from Others

Accepting bullying from others is a troubling consequence of normalizing family bullying. When individuals grow up in environments where bullying is considered a part of everyday life, they may unknowingly carry this belief into their adult relationships. This can manifest in various ways, including tolerating mistreatment from friends, romantic partners, or colleagues.

One reason for this acceptance may be the normalization of bullying as a standard interpersonal dynamic. Individuals may believe that conflict and mistreatment are inherent in relationships, leading them to tolerate abusive behavior. Additionally, those who have experienced family bullying may internalize the belief that they deserve mistreatment, further perpetuating a cycle of accepting bullying from others.

Breaking free from this pattern of accepting mistreatment is essential for personal growth and well-being. Recognizing the impact of family bullying and seeking support, such as therapy or counseling, can help individuals understand their worth and develop healthier boundaries in their relationships. By learning to value themselves and assert their right to respectful treatment, they can break free from the cycle of accepting bullying from others and create healthier, more empowering connections.

Passing On The Behavior

Passing on the behavior of bullying is a distressing consequence of family bullying normalization. Those who have experienced bullying within their own families may inadvertently perpetuate these harmful behaviors in their relationships, compounding the cycle of abuse.

One reason for this perpetuation is the flawed belief that bullying is a means of asserting control or protecting oneself. Individuals who have been victims of family bullying may erroneously internalize these tactics as effective ways of dealing with conflict or vulnerability. This learned behavior can lead to the repetition of bullying in their interactions with friends, partners, or even their children.

Moreover, unresolved trauma from their own experiences of family bullying may play a significant role in this pattern. Individuals who have not processed their trauma may unconsciously use bullying as a coping mechanism, mistakenly believing it provides a sense of control or safety.

Breaking this cycle requires a profound commitment to self-awareness, healing, and personal growth. Seeking therapy or counseling can be instrumental in addressing the root causes of these behaviors and learning healthier ways of relating to others. It's essential to recognize that perpetuating bullying harms others and perpetuates a legacy of pain and trauma that can span generations. Breaking free from this cycle is vital to healing and fostering healthier relationships.

Recognizing And Breaking The Cycle

Recognizing and breaking the cycle of self-perpetuated bullying is a crucial step toward healing and personal growth. It begins with self-awareness and a genuine commitment to change.

The first pivotal moment comes when individuals acknowledge the harmful impact of their behaviors on themselves and others. This recognition can be challenging but is essential for fostering empathy and understanding. It's an acknowledgment that bullying, in any form, is detrimental to the victims and the perpetrator's well-being.

Once this awareness takes root, the next step is actively seeking healthier ways to relate to others. This often involves seeking professional help, such as therapy or counseling, to address the root causes of the bullying behaviors. Therapy can provide the necessary tools and insights to break free from the cycle and develop healthier communication and coping mechanisms.

Additionally, individuals must commit to self-reflection and personal growth. This may entail challenging deeply ingrained beliefs and thought patterns, learning how to manage anger and frustration, and building emotional intelligence. It's an ongoing journey that requires dedication and resilience.

Breaking the cycle of self-perpetuated bullying is not only an act of self-compassion but also a profound transformation that allows individuals to lead healthier, more fulfilling lives and build positive, nurturing relationships with others.

Freedom In Breaking the Cycle

Healing And Growth

Breaking the cycle of normalized family bullying is a transformative journey that paves the way for healing and personal growth. This pivotal step marks a profound shift from perpetuating harm to actively seeking positive change.

Healing begins with acknowledging the wounds inflicted by bullying within the family. It's an opportunity to confront unresolved trauma and emotional scars that may have been carried for years. By facing these painful experiences head-on, individuals can start mending and finding closure.

Moreover, breaking the cycle empowers individuals to cultivate healthier patterns of communication and interaction. It involves learning effective conflict resolution skills, practicing empathy and active listening, and fostering a deeper understanding of oneself and others. These newfound abilities contribute to developing nurturing relationships within the family and in other areas of life.

As healing progresses, personal growth unfolds. Individuals discover their inner strength, resilience, and capacity for change. They gain a greater sense of self-worth and self-compassion, which fuels their journey towards becoming the best versions of themselves.

In essence, breaking free from the cycle of normalized family bullying is an act of self-liberation, enabling individuals to heal, grow, and build a future marked by healthier relationships and personal fulfillment. It's a testament to the human spirit's remarkable ability to transform adversity into strength and light.

Healthy Relationships

Breaking free from the cycle of normalized family bullying paves the way for cultivating healthy and meaningful relationships. It marks a crucial turning point in one's life, where individuals can unlearn harmful behaviors and embrace a new way of connecting with others.

One of the critical transformations is the ability to assert oneself without resorting to bullying tactics. Individuals who have broken free from the cycle understand the importance of clear communication and boundary-setting. They recognize that respect for oneself and others is the foundation of any healthy relationship.

Trust becomes a cornerstone in these new connections. By breaking the cycle, individuals demonstrate their commitment to honesty and authenticity in their interactions. This builds trust among friends, partners, and loved ones, creating an atmosphere of safety and emotional intimacy.

Healthy relationships also thrive on mutual respect. Those who have overcome the normalization of family bullying understand the significance of respecting others' boundaries, opinions, and feelings. This newfound respect enhances the quality of their relationships and fosters deeper connections with people who value and reciprocate this respect.

In essence, breaking free from family bullying's grip opens the door to a world of healthy, nurturing relationships. It's a journey that empowers individuals to build connections based on trust, respect, and open communication, ultimately leading to a happier and more fulfilling life surrounded by people who uplift and support them.

Empowerment

Empowerment is the radiant result of breaking free from the cycle of normalized family bullying. It's the feeling of taking control of one's life and relationships, where individuals become the architects of their destiny.

By breaking the cycle, individuals gain the power to define their boundaries and expectations. They no longer tolerate disrespectful or harmful behavior, setting a clear standard for how they deserve to be treated. This newfound self-worth acts as a guiding light in all their interactions.

Assertiveness becomes a valuable skill in this journey. Those who have broken free understand the importance of asserting their needs and desires while respecting the autonomy of others. They confidently communicate, knowing they have the right to express themselves without resorting to bullying tactics.

Empowerment also extends to making choices that align with their well-being. Individuals who have overcome family bullying take charge of their lives, pursuing paths that nurture their growth and happiness. They no longer allow the fear of conflict or the normalization of mistreatment to hold them back.

In essence, breaking the cycle of family bullying empowers individuals to lead lives filled with self-respect, assertiveness, and the freedom to make choices that honor their authentic selves. It's a transformation that allows them to embrace their worth and create relationships and experiences that truly empower them.

The normalization of bullying within families is a complex issue with far-reaching consequences. It impacts how individuals relate to others, often leading to overly aggressive or isolated behavior, a fear of conflict, and a reluctance to tell the truth. Moreover, some individuals may perpetuate the cycle of bullying in their relationships.

Breaking this cycle is a transformative process that requires self-awareness, healing, and a commitment to change. However, the freedom gained from breaking free from the normalization of family bullying is immeasurable. It leads to healthier relationships, personal growth, and empowerment, allowing individuals to build a brighter and more respectful future for themselves and those they interact with.

Honest Inner Reflection for Healing

I n the bustling landscape of our lives, amidst the ebb and flow of responsibilities, emotions, and interactions, a sacred space can be our compass, confidant, and catalyst for healing – the realm of journaling and honest inner reflection. In pursuing healing, understanding, and growth, these practices stand as pillars of self-discovery, inviting us to embark on a journey transcending time and circumstance.

A Canvas for Self-Expression

A journal is more than just a collection of words on paper; it is an intimate gateway into the recesses of our hearts and minds. It is a sanctuary where we can unveil our deepest thoughts, untangle the complexities of our emotions, and chronicle the experiences in our lives. Whether through handwritten scrawls or typed entries, journaling provides a canvas for self-expression that transcends judgment, enabling us to embrace the full spectrum of our feelings – the joy, the pain, the uncertainties, and the triumphs.

In the context of healing, consistent journaling becomes a reliable companion on our path to recovery. It captures the nuances of our experiences, allowing us to revisit and reflect upon our journey from a distance. This act of revisitation is where the true magic happens – we see our evolution, our resilience, and the patterns that once bound us to our wounds. By putting our thoughts to paper, we acknowledge their existence and create a tangible record of our growth.

Mirrors Of Self-Discovery

Honest inner reflection is gazing into the mirrors of our minds and souls, peeling away the layers of pretense and denial to reveal our authentic selves. It's about having the courage to confront our thoughts, beliefs, and behaviors with an unwavering commitment to truth. This practice involves delving into the shadows, where our vulnerabilities reside, and shedding light on the unexamined corners of our being.

In healing, honest inner reflection acts as a spotlight, illuminating the root causes of our pain and struggles. It unveils the hidden narratives we tell ourselves, the limiting beliefs that hold us back, and the unresolved emotions that linger beneath the surface. By confronting these aspects, we can rewrite our story – to replace self-doubt with self-compassion and pain with understanding.

The Symbiosis Of Journaling And Reflection

The symbiotic relationship between consistent journaling and honest inner reflection forms a powerful union that propels our healing journey. Journaling provides the canvas upon which we pour our thoughts, emotions, and experiences. It is the act of release, a catharsis that unburdens our minds. In turn, honest inner reflection is the lens through which we examine those entries. The bridge connects our past, present, and future selves, allowing us to make sense of our experiences and uncover the threads that weave our narratives together.

Through this interplay, we learn to decode the messages hidden within our words – the recurring patterns, the moments of clarity, and the pivotal turning points. Our journal entries become the breadcrumbs that lead us back to our truth, guiding us toward the revelations at the core of our healing process.

Embracing Transformation Through Self-Awareness

As we embark on the journey of consistent journaling and honest inner reflection, we are, in essence, embarking on a journey of self-awareness. This path invites us to acknowledge our wounds without judgment, embrace our growth with humility, and cultivate a deeper connection with our inner selves.

Through this process, we unlock the door to profound healing and transformation. We peel away the layers that no longer serve us, freeing ourselves from the grip of old wounds and self-imposed limitations. Consistent documenting our thoughts and engaging in honest inner reflection is an act of self-love, a gesture that tells us we are worth the time and effort it takes to nurture our well-being.

In the end, journaling and inner reflection are not mere activities; they are acts of empowerment that invite us to step into the role of our healers. They provide the tools to understand, to process, and to grow. They teach us that our stories are not set in stone but living narratives that can be shaped, reshaped, and ultimately transformed.

So, pick up that pen, open that notebook, and step into self-discovery. Remember that you are sowing the seeds of healing as you chronicle your experiences, thoughts, and emotions. With every word you write and every moment of reflection you engage in, you are laying the foundation for a journey of growth, empowerment, and the profound transformation of your heart and soul.

Best Practices For Journaling With A Busy Schedule

In the whirlwind of modern life, finding time for introspection and self-care can be challenging, especially when faced with a busy schedule. However, journaling remains a valuable tool for personal growth and healing, even amidst the chaos. By implementing a few strategic practices, you can harness the power of journaling to navigate your busy life while nurturing your emotional well-being.

Embrace Micro-Journaling

When time is scarce, micro-journaling can be a game-changer. Instead of committing to lengthy entries, jot down quick notes, bullet points, or even a sentence that captures your thoughts and feelings. These bite-sized reflections can be done on-the-go and accumulated over time to offer a snapshot of your journey.

Choose Consistency Over Length

The beauty of journaling lies in consistency, not in the length of each entry. Set aside a few minutes each day or every other day to write a brief entry. Consistency fosters a habit that becomes easier to maintain, even in the busiest schedules.

Integrate Journaling Into Your Routine

Incorporate journaling into existing routines, such as during your morning coffee, before bed, or during your commute (if you're not driving). By tying journaling to an existing habit, it becomes easier to remember and prioritize.

Keep A Journal Handy

Carry a small notebook or use a note-taking app on your phone to capture thoughts on the fly. This lets you seize spare moments throughout the day – waiting in line, during breaks, or for a meeting to start.

Set Realistic Expectations

Release the pressure of writing a masterpiece every time you journal. Some entries may be short, simple, or focused on a specific emotion or event. The goal is to capture your thoughts and feelings rather than to craft a flawless narrative.

Blend Journaling With Self-Care

Combine journaling with another self-care activity you already engage in. You can journal after your workout, meditation, or tea. This way, you're integrating self-reflection seamlessly into your routine.

Prioritize Intuition

Don't overthink your entries. Let your thoughts flow without worrying about structure or grammar. This unfiltered approach often leads to more genuine and insightful reflections.

Nurturing Yourself Amidst The Hustle

Incorporating journaling into a busy schedule is a powerful act of self-care. By embracing micro-journaling, consistency, prompts, and integrating journaling into your routine, you create an avenue for self-expression, reflection, and healing. Remember that the quality of your entries matters less than the consistency and intention behind them. In a world that seems to move at lightning speed, journaling offers you a moment of stillness, a refuge for your thoughts, and a way to prioritize your emotional well-being amidst the hustle and bustle of life.

So, pick up your pen and let it dance across the pages. Let the ink weave a tapestry of healing and empowerment—an intimate conversation with yourself that leads to renewal. Embrace the transformative power of journaling and step into a future where you stand tall, unburdened by the weight of wounds, and radiate with the radiance of self-love and the beauty of your unique journey.

I Forgive You For The Emotional And Psychological Manipulation

Forgiveness Morning Reflection of the Day

Forgiving the bullies in my family for their emotional and psychological manipulation is a profound journey toward my healing and liberation. In this process, I recognize that forgiveness doesn't condone their actions; instead, it sets me free from the shackles of resentment and anger their behavior has placed upon my heart.

Forgiveness is not about excusing or forgetting their actions but releasing the heavy burden of carrying their toxicity within me. By forgiving, I am choosing to prioritize my well-being over holding onto bitterness. I acknowledge that these bullies might be wounded themselves, projecting their pain onto others. Compassion, rather than vengeance, becomes my guiding light.

Forgiving them does not mean allowing them back into my life or enabling their behavior. It's about detaching from their power over my emotions. Forgiveness becomes an act of empowerment, a declaration that their actions will no longer define my emotional state.

Through forgiveness, I am cultivating emotional resilience. I am making space for healing, growth, and authentic happiness. This forgiveness is a gift I give to myself, not them. Reclaiming my emotional autonomy and rising above their manipulation is a conscious choice.

Forgiveness is a step towards breaking the cycle of pain that may have been perpetuated through generations. It is a radical act of self-love and an investment in my own mental and emotional freedom. In forgiving them, I am unburdening myself and creating a legacy of strength, compassion, and transformation.

Ultimately, forgiveness is a journey that takes time. It's about acknowledging my emotions, honoring my pain, and consciously releasing it. In letting go, I am embracing a future unburdened by the weight of their manipulation, allowing space for healing, joy, and the power to shape my narrative.

Meditative Healing Thought of the Day

As I release the hold that bullies in my family have had over me, I step into a realm of freedom. With each step away from their power, I free myself from their emotional clutches.

Deeper Connection Within

1. What emotions do I experience when family members bully me or cross my boundaries?

_____

_____

_____

_____

_____

_____

2. How have past experiences with family members influenced my current interactions?

_____

_____

_____

_____

_____

_____

3. What beliefs about myself might contribute to my difficulty enforcing boundaries?

_____

_____

_____

_____

_____

_____

Loving Statements About Me

I am the author of my own story and create a narrative of growth and empowerment.

I can face my fears and step out of my comfort zone.

I believe in my potential and my ability to achieve my goals.

Gratitude Reflection of the Day

Today, I am grateful for the person I have become—a resilient and loving individual who has embarked on a profound journey of healing and self-discovery.

Inner Reflections

I Forgive You For Protecting Harmful Secrets

Forgiveness Morning Reflection of the Day

Forgiving the bullies in my family for protecting harmful secrets is a profound act of reclaiming my emotional freedom. As I embark on this journey of forgiveness, I understand that their choice to shield these secrets doesn't define my worth nor justify their actions. Forgiveness is not a validation of their behavior but a release of the emotional burden they've unwittingly placed upon me.

Through forgiveness, I am choosing to break free from the chains of their secrecy. I recognize their actions were born from their struggles and fears, even if misguided. Forgiveness is my way of untangling myself from their web of concealment and deceit. By forgiving, I am no longer letting their choices imprison my emotions.

This act of forgiveness doesn't absolve them of responsibility; it allows me to regain control over my emotions. As I release the grip of resentment, I am paving the way for my healing. I am letting go of the weight their secrecy imposed on my heart.

Forgiveness empowers me to rise above their actions. It gives me the power to transcend their manipulative intentions and create a space for authenticity and truth. I acknowledge that their secrets are not mine to carry.

Forgiving them is an act of self-compassion. It's a declaration that I am worthy of emotional liberation, that I deserve to let go of the pain their secrets have caused. Forgiveness is not an overnight process; it's a journey I undertake with courage and determination.

I am making space for my growth and healing by choosing to forgive. It's a step towards rewriting my narrative, unburdened by their choices. Through forgiveness, I am forging a path to wholeness and reclaiming the power their secrets once stole from me.

Meditative Healing Thought of the Day

I am redefining my sense of self by breaking the chains that once bound me to their hurtful actions. I am embracing the power to chart my emotional course.

Deeper Connection Within

1. What story do I tell myself about why I don't stand up for myself?

_____

_____

_____

_____

_____

_____

2. How does allowing bullying align with my self-image and sense of identity?

_____

_____

_____

_____

_____

_____

3. What fears or anxieties arise when I consider asserting boundaries with my family?

_____

_____

_____

_____

_____

_____

Loving Statements About Me

I forgive myself for not always knowing how to handle difficult situations.

I release the weight of self-blame and embrace self-compassion.

I am human and deserving of forgiveness, including from myself.

Gratitude Reflection of the Day

I appreciate the moments when I've embraced self-love and self-appreciation, understanding that I am worthy of love and kindness from myself and others.

Inner Reflections

I Forgive You For Exposing My Private Experiences Without My Consent

Forgiveness Morning Reflection of the Day

Forgiving the bullies in my family for exposing my private experiences without my consent is a profound step towards reclaiming my autonomy and emotional well-being. As I embark on this journey of forgiveness, I acknowledge that their actions were a breach of trust and a violation of my boundaries. However, forgiveness is my pathway to liberation, a choice I make for myself, not for them.

By forgiving, I am releasing the grip of anger and hurt that their actions have had on my heart. Forgiveness does not minimize the impact of their behavior; instead, it empowers me to rise above it. It's a decision to prioritize my emotional health over the weight of their betrayal.

Forgiveness is a declaration that I no longer allow their actions to control my emotions. It's my way of reclaiming the narrative of my life and refusing to be defined by their choices. Through forgiveness, I no longer choose to be a victim of their actions.

This act of forgiveness doesn't mean condoning their behavior. It means acknowledging their flaws and choosing to release the resentment that has been holding me captive. Forgiveness is a courageous step towards breaking free from the chains of their betrayal.

As I forgive, I am also permitting myself to heal. Forgiveness is a gift I give to myself, allowing me to move forward with a lighter heart and a renewed sense of inner peace. It's about letting go of the pain their actions have caused me and allowing space for my growth and happiness.

In forgiving them, I am demonstrating my strength and resilience. I am taking back control over my emotions and my life. Forgiveness is not forgetting; it's choosing to live without the burden of their actions weighing me down. I am rewriting my empowerment, healing, and emotional liberation story through forgiveness.

Meditative Healing Thought of the Day

Their hurtful words or actions no longer define me. My identity is no longer tethered to their expectations. I am claiming my true self back.

Deeper Connection Within

1. How has my upbringing or childhood environment affected my perspective on boundaries?

_____

_____

_____

_____

_____

_____

2. Do I associate any positive or negative outcomes with not enforcing boundaries?

_____

_____

_____

_____

_____

_____

3. How do I imagine my life would change if I could set and maintain boundaries confidently?

_____

_____

_____

_____

_____

_____

Loving Statements About Me

My past does not define my worth; I can create my future.

I am healing, embracing every step with love and understanding.

I am allowed to let go of mistakes and move forward with grace.

Gratitude Reflection of the Day

I'm thankful for the capacity to nurture a sense of inner peace and self-acceptance, welcoming these qualities into my life with open arms.

Inner Reflections

I Forgive You For "Turning A Blind Eye" To Protect Predators

Forgiveness Morning Reflection of the Day

Forgiving the bullies in my family for "turning a blind eye" to protecting family predators is a profound act of emotional release and self-empowerment. Their complicity in the face of such harm is a betrayal of trust, but forgiveness is my choice to liberate myself from the weight of their indifference.

By forgiving, I am not absolving them of their responsibility or excusing their actions. Instead, I am choosing to transcend the darkness they contributed to and reclaim my sense of moral integrity. Forgiveness is my path to overcoming their silence and regaining control over my emotional well-being.

Through forgiveness, I am releasing the grip of resentment and anger that their inaction has held on my heart. Their behavior reflects their fears, insecurities, and inability to confront brutal truths. Forgiveness is a way of freeing myself from their limitations.

Forgiving them is an assertion of my power. It's a declaration that I refuse to be defined by their actions and attitudes. By forgiving, I acknowledge that their choices do not determine my self-worth but my ability to heal and grow.

This act of forgiveness doesn't erase the pain or the trauma. Instead, it allows me to channel my energy into healing and well-being. I am choosing to let go of the emotional burden they've placed upon me and find solace in my strength.

Forgiveness is not a sign of weakness; it's a testament to my resilience. It's about taking back the control they tried to take from me. Through forgiveness, I am stepping into the light of my truth, leaving behind their shadows of neglect and indifference.

Meditative Healing Thought of the Day

I rise above the negativity they once projected onto me—my spirit soars, free from the weight of their judgments. I am a force of positivity.

Deeper Connection Within

1. How do I prioritize others' feelings and needs over my own?

_____
_____
_____
_____
_____
_____

2. What behavior patterns in my family might contribute to this dynamic?

_____
_____
_____
_____
_____
_____

3. How have roles and expectations within my family affected my willingness to enforce boundaries?

_____
_____
_____
_____
_____
_____

Loving Statements About Me

I deserve self-love and forgiveness just as much as anyone else.

Each moment is an opportunity to show kindness to myself, no matter what has happened.

I acknowledge my growth and progress, celebrating every step toward self-forgiveness.

Gratitude Reflection of the Day

I appreciate the times when I've let go of self-criticism and self-doubt, recognizing that they no longer have a place in my heart.

Inner Reflections

I Forgive Myself For Allowing You To Silence My Voice

Forgiveness Morning Reflection of the Day

Forgiving myself for allowing the bullies in my family to silence my voice is a profound act of self-compassion and personal growth. It's an acknowledgment that I was navigating challenging circumstances with the tools I had at the time. Forgiveness is a step towards releasing the self-blame and embracing the healing path.

By forgiving myself, I am honoring my journey and the survival mechanisms I employed. I recognize that I may have silenced my voice to protect myself from further harm. Forgiveness is a way of showing kindness to the person I was then and the person I am now.

Through forgiveness, I am breaking the cycle of self-criticism and self-judgment. I am letting go of the heavy burden of guilt and embracing the opportunity to rewrite my narrative. Forgiveness is an act of reclamation; it's a decision to take back the power that was once relinquished.

Forgiving myself doesn't negate the pain or the experiences I endured. Instead, it's about understanding that healing is a nonlinear journey, and I am allowed to give myself grace along the way. By forgiving, I am creating space for self-love and self-acceptance to flourish.

This act of forgiveness is a commitment to my well-being. It's about nurturing my emotional growth and allowing me to find my voice again. Through forgiveness, I am embracing the lessons I've learned and using them to empower my present and shape my future.

Forgiving myself is an act of strength. It's a decision to break free from the chains of the past and step into a realm of possibility and transformation. It's about recognizing that I deserve to be heard and have the power to reclaim my voice and narrative.

Meditative Healing Thought of the Day

Within me resides an oasis of calm and tranquility. As I untangle myself from their manipulation, I invite inner peace to wash over me like gentle waves.

I forgive myself for allowing you to silence my voice.

Deeper Connection Within

1. How do other family members react when I try to assert my boundaries?

_____

_____

_____

_____

_____

_____

2. What messages did I receive from my family about assertiveness and standing up for myself?

_____

_____

_____

_____

_____

_____

3. Are there any family norms that discourage open communication and boundary-setting?

_____

_____

_____

_____

_____

_____

Loving Statements About Me

I am deserving of my forgiveness and acceptance.

I am worthy of love and respect, starting with the love and respect I show myself.

I believe in my capabilities and dare to pursue my dreams.

Gratitude Reflection of the Day

Today, I'm sending gratitude to the support system that has helped me on my journey, whether it's family, friends, or mentors.

Inner Reflections

I Forgive You For Sweeping The Truth Under The Rug

Forgiveness Morning Reflection of the Day

Forgiving the bullies in my family for "sweeping the truth under the rug" is an act of profound emotional liberation and self-empowerment. Their choice to deny or hide the truth may have perpetuated pain and injustice, but forgiveness is my way of unburdening myself from their evasion and finding my path to healing.

By forgiving, I am not endorsing their actions or minimizing the impact of their choices. Instead, I choose to rise above their attempts to bury the truth. Forgiveness is my declaration that I refuse to let their silence dictate the trajectory of my emotional well-being.

Through forgiveness, I am relinquishing the heavy weight of resentment and frustration their actions have placed upon me. Their denial might be rooted in their fears and insecurities. Forgiveness is my means of breaking free from the cycle of hurt and rejection.

Forgiving them is a testament to my strength and resilience. It's a decision to embrace my truth and acknowledge the validity of my feelings. By forgiving, I assert my right to heal and move forward, regardless of their unwillingness to confront reality.

This act of forgiveness is a step towards creating my narrative. It's a conscious choice to free myself from the confines of their denial and claim my emotional sovereignty. I am opening the door to my growth and transformation through forgiveness.

Forgiving them is not an endorsement of their silence but a commitment to my well-being. It's about finding the power to heal despite their attempts to suppress the truth. Forgiveness is an act of reclamation, allowing me to move forward with authenticity, strength, and the belief that my voice and my truth matter.

Meditative Healing Thought of the Day

With their influence waning, I step into the spotlight of my self-confidence. I no longer seek validation from those who once undermined me.

Deeper Connection Within

1. What emotions arise when I consider the possibility of changing my family dynamic?

_____

_____

_____

_____

_____

_____

2. How might the power dynamics within my family influence my behavior and choices?

_____

_____

_____

_____

_____

_____

3. What unspoken agreements have I made with family members hinder boundary-setting?

_____

_____

_____

_____

_____

_____

Loving Statements About Me

Confidence flows through me naturally, empowering my actions and decisions.

I am strong and resilient, rising above challenges with confidence.

My unique qualities make me exceptional, and I confidently embrace them.

Gratitude Reflection of the Day

I'm grateful for the awareness that self-acceptance is a daily practice, and it's okay to take it one step at a time.

Inner Reflections

I Forgive You For Threatening To Walk Out Of My Life If I Didn't "Play By Your Rules"

Forgiveness Morning Reflection of the Day

Forgiving the bullies in my family for threatening to walk out of my life unless I conform to their terms is a courageous step towards my emotional liberation and self-worth. Their manipulation and conditional love may have left scars, but forgiveness is my way of reclaiming my power and breaking free from their emotional hold.

By forgiving, I am not endorsing their ultimatums or submitting to their control. Instead, I am choosing to release the emotional burden their threats have placed upon me. Forgiveness is my path to overcoming their attempts to coerce and assert dominance over my decisions and identity.

Through forgiveness, I am shedding the weight of fear and insecurity their threats instilled. I recognize that their actions stem from their insecurities and desire for control. Forgiveness is my declaration that their attempts to manipulate me will no longer define my sense of self-worth.

Forgiving them is an assertion of my autonomy. It's a testament to my resilience and commitment to honoring my truth. By forgiving, I am dismantling their power over my emotions and decisions.

This act of forgiveness is a journey towards self-discovery and authenticity. It's a conscious choice to prioritize my well-being over their conditional approval. Through forgiveness, I embrace that my value is not contingent upon their approval or presence.

Forgiving them doesn't mean forgetting the pain or dismissing their behavior. It's about choosing to heal and grow beyond their attempts to manipulate. Forgiveness is my way of forging a path to self-love, inner strength, and the unwavering belief that I deserve to live on my terms, free from threats and manipulation.

Meditative Healing Thought of the Day

The pain they caused me is transformed into a wellspring of resilience and strength. Each scar is a testament to my growth.

Deeper Connection Within

1. How does the concept of loyalty impact my decisions around enforcing boundaries?

_____

_____

_____

_____

_____

_____

2. Do I feel responsible for the well-being or happiness of my family members?

_____

_____

_____

_____

_____

_____

3. How do I perceive myself when I allow family members to bully me or disregard my boundaries?

_____

_____

_____

_____

_____

_____

Loving Statements About Me

I trust myself to make decisions that align with my best interests.

I am deserving of success, and I confidently pursue my goals.

I have the power to transform self-doubt into self-assuredness.

Gratitude Reflection of the Day

I appreciate the moments when I've celebrated my strengths and acknowledged my areas of growth, understanding that both are essential parts of my journey.

Inner Reflections

DAY 8

I Forgive You For Always Being The Victim And Refusing To Take Accountability For Your Actions

Forgiveness Morning Reflection of the Day

Forgiving the bullies in my family for their refusal to be accountable for their actions and behavior is a profound step toward my emotional emancipation and personal growth. Their unwillingness to acknowledge their wrongdoings might have caused frustration, but forgiveness is my pathway to release the weight of their lack of responsibility and regain control over my well-being.

By forgiving, I am not excusing their actions or permitting them to continue their behavior. Instead, I am choosing to unburden myself from the anger and resentment their lack of accountability has caused. Forgiveness is my means of setting myself free from the cycle of denial.

I prioritize my mental and emotional health through forgiveness over their refusal to confront the truth. Their avoidance might stem from their fears and insecurities. Forgiveness is my declaration that their actions will no longer dictate my emotional state.

Forgiving them is a testament to my strength and resilience. It's a decision to rise above their denial and take ownership of my healing. By forgiving, I assert my right to move forward and grow, regardless of their inability to take responsibility.

This act of forgiveness is a journey towards self-empowerment. It's a conscious choice to let go of their lack of accountability and embrace my capacity for healing. Through forgiveness, I am creating space for my transformation, where I am not defined by their actions but by my ability to overcome and thrive.

Forgiving them doesn't mean ignoring the pain or forgetting their behavior. It's about reclaiming my power, letting go of the emotional burden, and forging a future where my self-awareness and growth guide me.

Meditative Healing Thought of the Day

As I distance myself from their toxicity, I rebuild trust in my instincts. I trust myself to make choices aligned with my well-being.

Deeper Connection Within

1. What beliefs about my worthiness of respect and kindness contribute to my behavior?

_____

_____

_____

_____

_____

_____

2. Have there been instances in my past that reinforced the idea that my needs don't matter?

_____

_____

_____

_____

_____

_____

3. How does fear of rejection or abandonment affect my boundary-setting decisions?

_____

_____

_____

_____

_____

_____

Loving Statements About Me

I recognize my achievements and hold my head high with pride.

Every day, I grow more confident and assured in who I am.

I am worthy of setting boundaries that protect my well-being and happiness.

Gratitude Reflection of the Day

I'm thankful for the strength to choose self-acceptance over self-judgment, which leads me closer to inner peace.

Inner Reflections

I Forgive You For The Emotional Blackmail

Forgiveness Morning Reflection of the Day

Forgiving the bullies in my family for resorting to emotional blackmail when I told the truth is an act of profound self-compassion and resilience. Their manipulation and attempts to silence me might have caused deep wounds, but forgiveness is my way of reclaiming my voice and releasing the emotional shackles their tactics imposed.

By forgiving, I am not condoning their behavior or surrendering to their control. Instead, I am choosing to release the burden of anger and hurt that their emotional blackmail has placed upon my heart. Forgiveness is my pathway to take back control over my narrative and emotional well-being.

Through forgiveness, I am untangling myself from the grip of their manipulation. I understand their tactics are often born from their insecurities and fear of exposure. Forgiveness is my declaration that their attempts to silence me will no longer dictate the course of my life.

Forgiving them is an assertion of my inner strength. It's a testament to my resilience and a way of regaining my power. By forgiving, I rise above their attempts to suppress my truth and shape my story.

This act of forgiveness is a journey towards self-empowerment. It's a conscious decision to prioritize my emotional healing over their efforts to control my emotions. Through forgiveness, I am allowing myself to heal and grow beyond the scars of their manipulation.

Forgiving them doesn't mean ignoring the pain or pretending their behavior didn't hurt. It's about recognizing my worth, setting myself free from their emotional hold, and forging a future where I define my identity and speak my truth unapologetically.

Meditative Healing Thought of the Day

Radiating Empowerment: I am a beacon of empowerment, shining brightly against the darkness of their manipulation. My light guides me toward healing and self-love.

I forgive you for the emotional blackmail when I told the truth.

Deeper Connection Within

1. What core beliefs do I hold about conflict, confrontation, and its potential consequences?

_____

_____

_____

_____

_____

_____

2. Do I believe I deserve to be treated with respect and kindness by family members?

_____

_____

_____

_____

_____

_____

3. What emotions arise when I contemplate prioritizing my well-being?

_____

_____

_____

_____

_____

_____

Loving Statements About Me

My boundaries are a reflection of my self-worth and self-respect.

I trust myself to establish and maintain healthy boundaries with love and confidence.

I am strong enough to stand up for myself and communicate my needs.

Gratitude Reflection of the Day

Today, I'm sending thoughts of self-appreciation and self-love to my heart, honoring the unique and beautiful person I am.

Inner Reflections

I Forgive You For Excluding Me From The Family When I Didn't "Play By The Rules"

Forgiveness Morning Reflection of the Day

Forgiving the bullies in my family for excluding me when I refuse to adhere to their rules is a profound act of self-empowerment and emotional liberation. Their choice to isolate me as a form of control might have left scars, but forgiveness is my means of breaking free from their toxic dynamics and reclaiming my sense of belonging on my terms.

By forgiving, I am not endorsing their actions or surrendering my autonomy. Instead, I am choosing to release the weight of hurt and rejection their exclusion has placed upon me. Forgiveness is my path to regaining control over my emotional well-being and redefining my sense of belonging.

Through forgiveness, I am disentangling myself from their manipulative strategies. I acknowledge that their exclusionary tactics are rooted in their insecurities and need for dominance. Forgiveness is my declaration that their attempts to control my participation in the family will no longer dictate my self-worth.

Forgiving them is an assertion of my inner strength. It's a testament to my resilience and a way of reclaiming my right to a fulfilling and authentic life. By forgiving, I rise above their efforts to manipulate my sense of belonging and shape my narrative.

This act of forgiveness is a journey towards self-acceptance and empowerment. It's a conscious choice to prioritize my emotional healing over their conditional acceptance. Through forgiveness, I am giving myself permission to heal and grow beyond the wounds of their exclusion.

Forgiving them doesn't mean erasing the pain or overlooking their behavior. It's about recognizing my inherent worth, freeing myself from their emotional grasp, and forging a path to a future where I define my place based on my values and authenticity.

Meditative Healing Thought of the Day

I am cultivating emotional resilience, capable of withstanding their attempts to undermine me. My inner strength fortifies me.

I forgive you for excluding me from the family when I didn't "play by the rules."

Deeper Connection Within

1. How do societal or cultural expectations influence how I approach family relationships?

_____
_____
_____
_____
_____
_____

2. What is my definition of a healthy, respectful relationship, and how does it align with reality?

_____
_____
_____
_____
_____
_____

3. How might my lack of self-compassion impact my ability to establish boundaries?

_____
_____
_____
_____
_____
_____

Loving Statements About Me

I release the guilt associated with asserting my boundaries; they are necessary and valid.

I prioritize my comfort and well-being by setting clear boundaries.

I choose to surround myself with people who respect and honor my boundaries.

Gratitude Reflection of the Day

I appreciate the power of self-acceptance to foster authentic relationships and create space for love and understanding.

Inner Reflections

DAY 11

I Forgive You For Making Me Feel Guilty For Loving Family Members You Don't Like

Forgiveness Morning Reflection of the Day

Forgiving the bullies in my family for making me feel guilty for loving a family member others don't like is an act of profound self-compassion and emotional liberation. Their attempts to manipulate my feelings and loyalty might have caused inner turmoil, but forgiveness is my pathway to releasing the burden of guilt and reclaiming my authentic emotions.

By forgiving, I am not endorsing their judgment or relinquishing my right to love freely. Instead, I am choosing to untangle myself from the web of their manipulation and release the emotional weight they've imposed. Forgiveness is my way of taking back control over my emotions and decisions.

Through forgiveness, I am disentangling myself from their toxic influence. I recognize that their efforts to manipulate my affections may stem from their insecurities and agendas. Forgiveness is my declaration that their attempts to control my feelings will no longer hold sway over my heart.

Forgiving them is a declaration of my inner strength. It's a testament to my resilience and a way of reaffirming my right to love unconditionally. By forgiving, I rise above their efforts to dictate my emotions and shape my experiences.

This act of forgiveness is a journey towards self-discovery and authenticity. It's a conscious choice to prioritize my emotional well-being over their attempts to instill guilt. Through forgiveness, I am granting myself the freedom to embrace my feelings without reservation.

Forgiving them doesn't mean forgetting the pain or ignoring their behavior. It's about acknowledging my right to feel and love without restraint. It's a step towards reclaiming my emotional autonomy and forging a path to a future where I define my relationships based on my heart and values.

Meditative Healing Thought of the Day

With each step away from their influence, I am rewriting the narrative of my life. I am the author of my story, and my ending is a triumph.

Deeper Connection Within

1. How do I feel immediately after allowing a boundary to be crossed or bullying to occur?

_____

_____

_____

_____

_____

_____

2. What emotions arise when I consider advocating for myself and enforcing boundaries?

_____

_____

_____

_____

_____

_____

3. How do my emotional triggers influence my reactions to family members' behavior?

_____

_____

_____

_____

_____

_____

Loving Statements About Me

I control how I allow others to treat me and choose respect.

I am deserving of relationships that are built on mutual respect and understanding.

I am creating a safe space for my growth and happiness by setting boundaries.

Gratitude Reflection of the Day

I'm grateful for the times when I've chosen to be kind to myself, recognizing the profound healing it brings to my heart and soul.

Inner Reflections

I Forgive Myself For Allowing Your Emotional Manipulation When I Began To Pursue My Dreams

Forgiveness Morning Reflection of the Day

Forgiving the bullies in my family for their emotional manipulations when I embark on pursuing my dreams is an act of immense strength and self-liberation. Their attempts to undermine my aspirations might have caused doubt and turmoil, but forgiveness is my means of transcending their control and reclaiming my path to success.

By forgiving, I am not validating their tactics or relinquishing my right to follow my dreams. Instead, I am choosing to release the emotional weight of their manipulation and regain ownership over my aspirations. Forgiveness is my declaration that their efforts to dissuade me will not deter my determination.

Through forgiveness, I am disentangling myself from the grip of their negativity. I acknowledge that their manipulation is rooted in their fears and insecurities. Forgiveness is my assertion that their attempts to thwart my ambitions will no longer govern my choices.

Forgiving them is a testament to my resilience and commitment to self-discovery. It's a conscious choice to prioritize my dreams over their attempts to control my trajectory. By forgiving, I am rising above their influence and shaping my narrative of success.

This act of forgiveness is a journey towards self-empowerment and authenticity. It's about valuing my aspirations and permitting myself to pursue them despite their interference. Through forgiveness, I am dismantling their attempts to undermine my confidence.

Forgiving them doesn't mean forgetting the pain or ignoring their behavior. It's about recognizing my worth and determination. It's a step towards reclaiming my power and forging a future where my strength and resilience nurture my dreams.

Meditative Healing Thought of the Day

The layers of pretense they imposed are unraveling. I am embracing authenticity, revealing my true self without fear.

Deeper Connection Within

1. Do I use distraction or avoidance to cope with uncomfortable emotions?

_____

_____

_____

_____

_____

_____

2. What coping mechanisms do I employ when faced with family-related stress or conflict?

_____

_____

_____

_____

_____

_____

3. How do I communicate my feelings and needs to family members?

_____

_____

_____

_____

_____

_____

Loving Statements About Me

I forgive myself for not setting boundaries sooner and confidently create them now.

My journey of self-forgiveness and boundary-setting is a testament to my strength.

With self-forgiveness and confidence, I establish boundaries that honor my worth.

Gratitude Reflection of the Day

I appreciate the joy and lightness that self-love brings to my spirit and its positive impact on my relationships.

Inner Reflections

I Forgive Myself For Ignoring The Red Flags And Allowing You To Remain In My Personal Space

Forgiveness Morning Reflection of the Day

Forgiving the bullies in my family for ignoring the red flags and allowing me to remain in my personal space is an act of profound self-compassion and growth. Their lack of intervention in the face of harmful behavior may have caused distress. Still, forgiveness is my pathway to releasing the emotional burden and taking charge of my boundaries.

By forgiving, I am not validating their inaction or surrendering my right to a safe space. Instead, I am choosing to release the weight of disappointment and betrayal their negligence has placed upon me. Forgiveness is my way of regaining control over my boundaries and emotional well-being.

Through forgiveness, I am freeing myself from the grip of their choices. Their indifference might arise from their struggles and avoidance of brutal truths. Forgiveness is my declaration that their failure to protect my space will not define my sense of security.

Forgiving them is an affirmation of my strength and commitment to self-care. It's a testament to my resilience and decision to set my standards for personal boundaries. By forgiving, I am rising above their lack of involvement and shaping a future where my safety is a priority.

This act of forgiveness is a journey towards self-empowerment and self-protection. It's a conscious choice to prioritize my emotional well-being over their inability to act. I am reclaiming my agency and granting myself the right to a secure environment through forgiveness.

Forgiving them doesn't mean disregarding the pain or overlooking their behavior. It's about acknowledging my worth and taking steps to ensure my safety. It's a step towards reclaiming my personal space and forging a future where I am empowered to establish and maintain healthy boundaries.

Meditative Healing Thought of the Day

I honor the choices that lead me away from their grasp. With each decision rooted in self-love, I pave the path towards liberation.

Deeper Connection Within

1. What fears do I associate with expressing my genuine emotions in family interactions?

_____

_____

_____

_____

_____

_____

2. How do I differentiate between situations where boundaries should be set and those that may not be necessary?

_____

_____

_____

_____

_____

_____

3. How do my emotional responses align with my long-term well-being and self-respect?

_____

_____

_____

_____

_____

_____

Loving Statements About Me

I release the need to seek validation from family members; my confidence comes from within.

I am worthy of forgiveness, confidence, and respectful relationships.

Each step toward forgiveness and boundaries is a step toward my empowerment.

Gratitude Reflection of the Day

I'm thankful for the lessons I've learned through self-acceptance—lessons of compassion, empathy, and embracing imperfection.

Inner Reflections

I Forgive You For Never Seeing The Good In Me And Only Critizing My Decisions

Forgiveness Morning Reflection of the Day

Forgiving the bullies in my family for their consistent criticism and failure to see the good in me is an act of immense self-compassion and personal growth. Their negative judgment may have caused wounds, but forgiveness is my way of shedding the weight of their opinions and embracing my inherent worth.

I am not validating their hurtful behavior or diminishing my value by forgiving them. Instead, I am choosing to release the emotional burden of their criticism and regain control over my self-esteem. Forgiveness is my path to reclaiming my self-worth and confidence.

Through forgiveness, I am freeing myself from the grip of their negativity. Their critical nature might stem from their insecurities and projected fears. Forgiveness is my declaration that their inability to see my strengths will not determine my self-perception.

Forgiving them is a declaration of my inner strength and self-assurance. It's a testament to my resilience and a way of redefining my self-image. By forgiving, I rise above their judgments and shape a future where I define my value.

This act of forgiveness is a journey towards self-acceptance and self-love. It's a conscious choice to prioritize my emotional well-being over their toxic opinions. Through forgiveness, I am granting myself the freedom to be authentically me without seeking their approval.

Forgiving them doesn't mean disregarding the pain or ignoring their behavior. It's about recognizing my worth and affirming their criticism does not define me. It's a step towards reclaiming my self-esteem and forging a future where I embrace my strengths and live confidently and self-assuredly.

Meditative Healing Thought of the Day

Cultivating Boundaries: I am cultivating boundaries that safeguard my emotions and well-being. These boundaries are a shield of self-respect against their negativity.

I forgive you for never seeing the good in me and only criticizing my decisions.

Deeper Connection Within

1. Do I prioritize short-term peace over my long-term emotional health?

_____
_____
_____
_____
_____
_____

2. What would benefit from breaking free from the pattern of allowing bullying and not enforcing boundaries?

_____
_____
_____
_____
_____

3. What steps have I taken in the past to address this issue, and what were the outcomes?

_____
_____
_____
_____
_____
_____

Loving Statements About Me

I lovingly let go of the past and embrace the confident, boundary-setting person I am becoming.

My boundaries reflect my self-love and my commitment to my well-being.

I deserve positive, respectful interactions, and I hold that truth.

Gratitude Reflection of the Day

Today, I'm sending loving energy to myself, expressing gratitude for my resilience and the growth I've experienced.

Inner Reflections

I Forgive My Mind For Believing I Had To Put Up With The Toxic Behavior To Prove My Family Loyalty

Forgiveness Morning Reflection of the Day

Forgiving the bullies in my family for making me believe I had to endure toxic behavior to prove my loyalty is a profound act of self-compassion and personal transformation. Their manipulation of my sense of loyalty may have caused deep confusion. Still, forgiveness is my way of releasing the chains that bound me to their toxic patterns and reclaiming my autonomy.

By forgiving, I am not validating their harmful perspective or forfeiting my right to self-respect. Instead, I am choosing to let go of the emotional burden their beliefs placed upon me. Forgiveness is my path to recognizing my worth and breaking free from the false narrative of loyalty they imposed.

Through forgiveness, I am freeing myself from their web of control. Their distorted values shaped their perspective. Forgiveness is my declaration that their toxic expectations will not dictate my choices or self-worth.

Forgiving them is a testament to my strength and self-awareness. It's a declaration that their toxic definitions of loyalty no longer bind me. By forgiving, I am stepping out of the shadows of their control and forging a new narrative for my life.

This act of forgiveness is a journey towards self-discovery and empowerment. It's a conscious choice to prioritize my emotional well-being over their distorted expectations. Through forgiveness, I am granting myself the freedom to define loyalty in a way that aligns with my values and self-respect.

Forgiving them doesn't mean forgetting the pain or ignoring their behavior. It's about recognizing my autonomy and affirming that I can be loyal to myself and my well-being. It's a step towards reclaiming my identity and forging a path to a future where my loyalty is directed toward my growth and happiness.

Meditative Healing Thought of the Day

Guilt loses its grip on me as I realize I can prioritize my happiness. I release the burden of pleasing them at my expense.

Deeper Connection Within

1. What support systems do I have in place that could assist me in asserting boundaries?

_____

_____

_____

_____

_____

_____

2. How do I envision my life-changing if I confidently enforce boundaries with my family?

_____

_____

_____

_____

_____

_____

3. What personal strengths and resources can I draw upon to help me in this process?

_____

_____

_____

_____

_____

_____

Loving Statements About Me

Through self-forgiveness, confidence, and boundary-setting, I am rewriting my story.

I am curious and eager to learn more about myself and the world.

I have the inner resources to navigate any situation that comes my way.

Gratitude Reflection of the Day

I appreciate the opportunities to practice self-love daily, as it is a transformative practice that enriches every aspect of my life.

Inner Reflections

I Forgive You For Guilting And Shaming Me For Saying "No"

Forgiveness Morning Reflection of the Day

Forgiving the bullies in my family for guilting and shaming me for saying no is an act of profound self-empowerment and emotional liberation. Their manipulation and attempts to undermine my boundaries may have caused internal conflict. Still, forgiveness is my pathway to releasing the burden of guilt and reclaiming my right to set healthy limits.

By forgiving, I am not endorsing their tactics or surrendering my right to assert myself. Instead, I am choosing to let go of the emotional weight their guilt and shame tactics have imposed. Forgiveness is my way of redefining my self-worth and standing firm in my decisions.

Through forgiveness, I am disentangling myself from their control. Their manipulative behavior may stem from their desire for power and dominance. Forgiveness is my declaration that their attempts to make me feel guilty for setting boundaries will no longer dictate my choices.

Forgiving them is an affirmation of my strength and autonomy. It's a testament to my resilience and my commitment to self-care. By forgiving, I overcame their efforts to undermine my confidence in saying no.

This act of forgiveness is a journey towards self-respect and authenticity. It's a conscious choice to prioritize my emotional well-being over their attempts to manipulate my boundaries. I am reclaiming my power to make choices that align with my needs and values through forgiveness.

Forgiving them doesn't mean ignoring the pain or dismissing their behavior. It's about recognizing my worth and asserting I can say no without guilt or shame. It's a step towards reclaiming my autonomy and forging a future where I honor my boundaries confidently and self-assuredly.

Meditative Healing Thought of the Day

With their influence fading, I am enveloped in self-love like a warm embrace. I nourish my spirit with the care I once withheld.

Deeper Connection Within

1. How might learning to enforce boundaries positively impact other areas of my life?

_____

_____

_____

_____

_____

_____

2. What have I learned about myself from past attempts (successful or not) at boundary-setting?

_____

_____

_____

_____

_____

_____

3. How can I cultivate self-compassion and patience as I work on this aspect of personal growth?

_____

_____

_____

_____

_____

_____

Loving Statements About Me

I am the author of my own story and create a narrative of growth and empowerment.

I can face my fears and step out of my comfort zone.

I believe in my potential and my ability to achieve my goals.

Gratitude Reflection of the Day

I'm grateful for the inner strength that self-acceptance fosters, allowing me to navigate life's challenges with grace and confidence.

Inner Reflections

I Forgive You For Always Throwing My Past Mistakes In My Face When I Speak Of Moving On

Forgiveness Morning Reflection of the Day

Forgiving the bullies in my family for consistently using my past mistakes against me when I try to move forward is a profound act of self-compassion and personal growth. Their continuous reminders of my errors may have caused pain and hindered my progress. Still, forgiveness is my way of shedding the weight of their manipulation and embracing my healing journey.

By forgiving, I am not validating their hurtful behavior or negating my efforts to grow. Instead, I am choosing to release the emotional burden their actions have placed upon me. Forgiveness is my pathway to freeing myself from the shackles of their judgment and regaining my inner strength.

Through forgiveness, I am liberating myself from their control. Their actions might stem from their insecurities or the desire to maintain a sense of power. Forgiveness is my declaration that their attempts to hold me back from my past mistakes will not define my future potential.

Forgiving them is a testament to my resilience and commitment to self-improvement. It's an affirmation of my worthiness of growth and personal transformation. By forgiving, I am rising above their attempts to anchor me in my past and shape my narrative of progress.

This act of forgiveness is a journey towards self-discovery and empowerment. It's a conscious choice to prioritize my emotional well-being over their attempts to hinder my growth. Through forgiveness, I am granting myself the freedom to move forward without the weight of their judgment.

Forgiving them doesn't mean ignoring the pain or dismissing their behavior. It's about recognizing my capacity to evolve and heal. It's a step towards reclaiming my growth journey and forging a path to a future where I embrace my potential with confidence and determination, unburdened by the weight of my past mistakes.

Meditative Healing Thought of the Day

I find a harmonious rhythm as I disconnect from their discordant energy. I resonate with the serenity of my soul.

I forgive you for always throwing my past mistakes in my face when I speak of moving on.

Deeper Connection Within

1. What small, gradual steps can I take to build confidence in asserting boundaries?

_____

_____

_____

_____

_____

_____

2. How can I remind myself of my progress and achievements along this journey?

_____

_____

_____

_____

_____

_____

3. How do I want to feel about myself when I think about how I handle family interactions?

_____

_____

_____

_____

_____

_____

Loving Statements About Me

I am open to change, and I welcome new experiences with enthusiasm.

I am constantly evolving and expanding my horizons.

I am open to receiving feedback and using it to improve myself.

Gratitude Reflection of the Day

I appreciate the moments when I've extended self-forgiveness and self-compassion to myself, recognizing that I deserve these gifts.

Inner Reflections

I Forgive You For The Hypocrisy And Double Standards

Forgiveness Morning Reflection of the Day

Forgiving the bullies in my family for their hypocrisy and double standards is an act of profound self-liberation and emotional healing. Their inconsistent behavior and unfair expectations may have caused frustration, but forgiveness is releasing the emotional burden and transcending their toxic patterns.

I am not endorsing their double standards or surrendering my principles by forgiving. Instead, I am choosing to let go of the resentment and disappointment their actions have instilled. Forgiveness is my path to freeing myself from their hypocrisy and reclaiming my sense of integrity.

Through forgiveness, I am disentangling myself from their web of inconsistency. Their behavior might be rooted in their confusion or insecurity. Forgiveness is my declaration that their double standards will not define my self-worth or moral compass.

Forgiving them is a testament to my strength and commitment to authenticity. It's a way of reaffirming my values and redefining my sense of self. By forgiving,

I rise above their behavior and shape my narrative of consistency and fairness.

This act of forgiveness is a journey towards self-respect and inner peace. It's a conscious choice to prioritize my emotional well-being over their toxic dynamics. Through forgiveness, I can maintain my standards regardless of their inconsistency.

Forgiving them doesn't mean ignoring the pain or dismissing their behavior. It's about recognizing my worth and affirming that I deserve to live by my values. It's a step towards reclaiming my integrity and forging a path to a future where I navigate life guided by my principles and self-respect.

Meditative Healing Thought of the Day

I welcome the freedom of detaching their emotions from mine. Their negativity no longer has the power to dictate my feelings.

Deeper Connection Within

1. What kind of relationship dynamics do I aspire to have with family members in the future?

_____

_____

_____

_____

_____

_____

2. How would I like to respond the next time a family member crosses a boundary?

_____

_____

_____

_____

_____

_____

3. What changes in my behavior and beliefs would align with the life I want to create?

_____

_____

_____

_____

_____

_____

Loving Statements About Me

I am committed to my growth journey and celebrate each step forward.

I embrace challenges as opportunities to learn and become stronger.

I am a beautiful soul, radiating love and positivity to the world.

Gratitude Reflection of the Day

I'm thankful for the peace and contentment that self-love and self-acceptance bring to my heart, creating a sanctuary of love.

Inner Reflections

I Forgive Myself For Giving You Chance After Chance When You Refuse To Change

Forgiveness Morning Reflection of the Day

Forgiving myself for giving my family a chance after chance, despite their refusal to change, is a decisive step toward my emotional liberation and self-growth. It's an acknowledgment that my intentions were based on hope and love, even if they were met with disappointment. Forgiveness is my pathway to release the self-blame and reclaim my emotional well-being.

By forgiving myself, I recognize my compassion and willingness to believe in the potential for change. I understand that my actions were driven by a genuine desire to see growth within my family. Forgiveness is a way of showing kindness to myself and acknowledging that change is a two-way process.

Through forgiveness, I am letting go of the weight of responsibility for their choices. I realize that change cannot be forced upon someone unwilling to embrace it. Forgiveness is my declaration that my worth is not tied to their actions or lack thereof.

Forgiving myself is a testament to my strength and capacity to learn from experiences. It's a conscious choice to prioritize my emotional well-being and growth over their behavior. By forgiving, I am taking back control over my emotions and my life.

This act of forgiveness is a journey towards self-empowerment and self-acceptance. It's about granting myself grace for my choices, even if they don't yield the desired outcome. Through forgiveness, I am opening the door to personal healing and growth, where I define my worth by my standards.

Forgiving myself doesn't mean forgetting the disappointment or ignoring the past. It's about recognizing my humanity and resilience. It's a step towards reclaiming my agency and forging a path to a future where I prioritize my growth and well-being, irrespective of others' choices.

Meditative Healing Thought of the Day

I choose empathy over resentment and strength over victimhood. I embody compassion for their struggles while forging my path.

Deeper Connection Within

1. How can I foster a sense of empowerment and assertiveness in my interactions?

_____

_____

_____

_____

_____

_____

2. What does a healthy version of me respond to discomfort?

_____

_____

_____

_____

_____

3. How do I see my self-worth evolving as I become more skilled at enforcing boundaries?

_____

_____

_____

_____

_____

Loving Statements About Me

I am allowed to set boundaries that protect my well-being and happiness.

I trust my intuition and make choices that align with my authentic self.

I release comparisons with others and embrace my unique journey.

Gratitude Reflection of the Day

Today, I'm sending kind and loving thoughts to myself, affirming that I am enough just as I am.

Inner Reflections

I Forgive Myself For Judging You For Never Taking The Advice You Give

Forgiveness Morning Reflection of the Day

Forgiving the bullies in my family for their hypocrisy in never following their advice and accusing me of "not listening" is an act of self-liberation and emotional healing. Their contradictory behavior and blame-shifting may have caused frustration, but forgiveness is my way of releasing the emotional burden and regaining my inner peace.

By forgiving, I am not endorsing their double standards or absolving them of their behavior. Instead, I am letting go of the resentment and confusion their actions have caused. Forgiveness is my path to reclaiming my emotional well-being and asserting my authenticity.

Through forgiveness, I am disentangling myself from the cycle of their inconsistency. Their accusations might be rooted in their inability to take responsibility for their actions. Forgiveness is my declaration that their shifting blame will no longer define my self-worth or ability to listen.

Forgiving them is a testament to my strength and commitment to my truth. It's a way of reaffirming my integrity and redefining my sense of self. By forgiving, I rise above their behavior and shape my narrative based on my experiences and observations.

This act of forgiveness is a journey toward self-respect and emotional freedom. It's a conscious choice to prioritize my well-being over their shifting perspectives. Through forgiveness, I am granting myself the permission to trust my judgment and value my ability to discern.

Forgiving them doesn't mean ignoring the pain or dismissing their behavior. It's about recognizing my worth and affirming that I deserve to be treated consistently and respectfully. It's a step towards reclaiming my self-assuredness and forging a path to a future where I navigate life guided by my insights and self-respect.

Meditative Healing Thought of the Day

Their attempts to dim my light are in vain. I shine with a brilliance that cannot be extinguished, basking in my radiance.

Deeper Connection Within

1. What role does self-forgiveness play in my journey to confidently assert boundaries?

_____

_____

_____

_____

_____

_____

2. How can I nurture a positive, respectful relationship with myself while working on this issue?

_____

_____

_____

_____

_____

_____

3. How do I imagine the conversations with my family members changing as I learn to enforce boundaries?

_____

_____

_____

_____

_____

_____

Loving Statements About Me

I treat myself with kindness and respect, just like a dear friend.

I am worthy of self-care and making my own needs a priority.

I am a valuable and irreplaceable presence in the lives of those who care about me.

Gratitude Reflection of the Day

I appreciate the courage it takes to embark on a journey of self-acceptance and self-love, and I celebrate the beautiful person I have become.

Inner Reflections

I Forgive You For The Physical And Verbal Aggression

Forgiveness Morning Reflection of the Day

Forgiving the bullies in my family for the physical, verbal, and emotional abuse is an incredibly complex and personal journey toward healing and self-empowerment. The wounds caused by their actions run deep, but forgiveness is a way of releasing the shackles of pain they imposed upon me and finding my path to emotional liberation.

I am not excusing their abusive behavior or condoning their actions by forgiving them. Instead, I am choosing to free myself from the emotional burden that their abuse has placed upon me. Forgiveness is my pathway to reclaiming my inner peace and regaining control over my emotional well-being.

Through forgiveness, I am disentangling myself from the grip of their toxicity. I understand their abuse might have reflected their unresolved issues and pain. Forgiveness is my declaration that their actions will not define my sense of self-worth or dictate my future.

Forgiving them is an act of tremendous courage and self-compassion. It's a testament to my resilience and a way of showing kindness to myself. By forgiving, I rise above the cycle of abuse and reclaim my strength and dignity.

This act of forgiveness is a journey towards self-healing and empowerment. It's a conscious choice to prioritize my emotional growth over their attempts to diminish me. Through forgiveness, I am granting myself the space to heal and rebuild my life on my terms.

Forgiving them doesn't mean forgetting the pain or overlooking their behavior. It's about recognizing my worth and affirming that I deserve to break free from the chains of their abuse. It's a step towards reclaiming my identity and forging a path to a future defined by my resilience, strength, and ability to heal.

Meditative Healing Thought of the Day

As I leave their shadow, I enter a new era of self-discovery and empowerment. I am the captain of my journey, charting a course towards freedom.

Deeper Connection Within

1. What emotions or thoughts come up when I imagine asserting a boundary with a family member who has bullied me in the past?

_____

_____

_____

_____

_____

2. Can I recall any specific experiences or events that have influenced my beliefs about asserting boundaries within my family?

_____

_____

_____

_____

_____

3. How do I perceive the concept of self-worth and self-respect in my family

dynamics?

_____

_____

_____

_____

_____

_____

Loving Statements About Me

Each day is a chance for a fresh start, and I embrace that opportunity.

I let go of self-blame and embrace self-love and acceptance.

I am allowed to make mistakes, and I am deserving of second chances.

Gratitude Reflection of the Day

I'm grateful for the opportunity to embrace healing, self-love, and self-appreciation in my family, creating a legacy of love and acceptance for future generations.

Inner Reflections

Reclaiming Your Power

Reclaiming your power is a testament to your unwavering commitment to self-discovery and growth. It acknowledges the pain you've carried, the wounds you've faced, and the strength that has emerged from within.

This journal has been your companion, offering a safe space to unearth buried emotions, release pent-up burdens, and reflect on your path to healing. It has encouraged you to confront the scars of family bullying, embrace forgiveness, and set boundaries that honor your well-being.

As you close this chapter of your journey, remember that healing is ongoing. Your story is one of resilience and transformation and continues evolving. The power to reclaim your life, unburdened by the past, rests firmly in your hands.

Your liberation is a testament to your strength, resilience, and capacity for growth. May the lessons learned within these pages accompany you on your journey toward a life filled with healing, forgiveness, and unwavering belief in your power.

The Key to Freedom

Forgiveness is the key to freedom from the chains of family bullying. It's a process of letting go, a profound self-compassion that allows you to break free from the cycle of hurt and resentment. By forgiving, you regain control of your life and redefine your narrative.

When you forgive, you no longer choose to be a prisoner of the past. You acknowledge that holding onto anger and pain only perpetuates the suffering. Instead, forgiveness empowers you to rise above the wounds and live a life that's not dictated by the actions of others.

It's essential to recognize that forgiveness is a gift you give to yourself. It liberates you from old grudges and opens the door to healing and growth. Through forgiveness, you transform your pain into strength, anger into compassion, and the past into a stepping stone toward a brighter future.

As you continue your journey of forgiveness and self-discovery, remember that you hold the key to your liberation. Your ability to forgive is a testament to your inner strength and commitment to creating a life defined by love, resilience, and freedom.

Empowering Your Self-Care

Setting healthy boundaries is an empowering act of self-care that you've cultivated on this transformative journey. You've recognized the importance of safeguarding your emotional and mental well-being through introspection and reflection. By setting boundaries, you've reclaimed your autonomy and affirmed your worth.

These boundaries protect against negativity and toxicity, allowing you to maintain emotional equilibrium. They act as a shield, ensuring that your needs, desires, and limits are respected. In doing so, you've created a space where your self-care thrives.

Setting boundaries is not about building walls but establishing clear and compassionate guidelines for how you wish to be treated and engage with the world. It's a powerful assertion of your self-worth and an affirmation that you deserve relationships and experiences that uplift and support you.

Remember that self-care is an ongoing practice as you continue to navigate your life with these newfound boundaries. A commitment to prioritizing your well-being and setting healthy boundaries is a cornerstone of that commitment. You've embarked on a journey of self-empowerment, and by honoring your limits, you're creating a life where your growth, happiness, and peace of mind flourish.

Reclaiming Your Emotional Freedom

Reclaiming your emotional freedom is a profound act of self-liberation. It signifies your refusal to be held hostage by family bullies' hurtful actions and words. By forgiving them, you break the chains that bound you to resentment and pain, freeing yourself from the burden of carrying their toxicity.

Through forgiveness, you acknowledge that their actions reflect their unhealed wounds and limitations, not a measure of your worth. You release the emotional weight that has held you captive, allowing space for healing and growth.

Setting healthy boundaries is another crucial step in reclaiming your emotional freedom. It empowers you to define how you wish to be treated and safeguards your mental and emotional well-being. By establishing these boundaries, you assert your right to live life on your terms, free from the intrusion of toxicity and negativity.

As you embark on this journey of self-discovery and healing, remember that your worthiness is innate. You are deserving of love, respect, and happiness. By forgiving and setting boundaries, you honor yourself and create a life that aligns with your true self.

Reclaiming your emotional freedom is not a one-time event; it's an ongoing process of self-care and self-empowerment. It's a commitment to nurturing your well-being and creating a life where you can thrive. Embrace this journey with courage and compassion, knowing you can break free from the past and step into a future filled with authenticity, resilience, and emotional liberation.

The Journey Ahead

The journey ahead is filled with opportunities for self-discovery and personal transformation. Remember that healing is not a linear path; there will be ups and downs. Embrace the lessons learned about forgiveness, setting healthy boundaries, and reclaiming your emotional freedom as guiding principles for your continued growth.

Stay connected to your inner strength and resilience, and draw upon the self-love and self-care practices you've cultivated. These will be your sources of sustenance and empowerment as you navigate the challenges that may arise.

Keep in mind that healing is not a destination but a lifelong journey. Embrace each day as an opportunity to learn, grow, and deepen your connection with yourself. Your experiences are a testament to your courage, and your story can inspire others to embark on their paths toward healing.

As you progress, continue to write your narrative with intention and purpose. You are the author of your life, and with each step, you shape a future defined by authenticity, self-love, and resilience.

May your journey ahead be filled with moments of self-discovery, joy, and empowerment. Remember that you can create a life that reflects your true self, liberated from the shackles of family bullying. The road may be winding, but it leads to a place of emotional freedom and empowerment that is entirely your own.

You Are Resilient. You Are Empowered. You Are Free.

You have shown incredible resilience throughout your journey, facing the shadows of family bullying with courage and determination. Your empowerment lies in your ability to forgive, set healthy boundaries, and reclaim your emotional freedom. These are not just tools; they are expressions of your inner strength.

As you move forward, remember that the past does not bind you. Your future is a canvas waiting for your creative touch. The scars and wounds you've faced are not limitations; they are reminders of your capacity to heal and grow.

You are free from the chains that once held you captive to the pain of family bullying. Your liberation is a beacon of hope for others on a similar path. Your journey inspires change and transformation within yourself, your community, and beyond.

Continue to nurture the self-love and self-care practices that have empowered you. They are the foundation of your emotional well-being. Embrace each day as an opportunity to explore your true self further, celebrate your victories, and learn from your challenges.

In closing, always remember these words:

You Are Resilient. You Are Empowered. You Are Free.

They are a declaration of your inner strength, your capacity for growth, and your unwavering worthiness of a life defined by authenticity, self-love, and empowerment.

May your future be filled with boundless possibilities, and may you continue to shine as a beacon of hope and inspiration for others on their journeys of healing and self-discovery.

Below Is A List Of All 35 Forgiveness Journals

Written By: Tuniscia Okeke

Available on Amazon and other major bookstores or www.forgivenesslifestyle.com
Instagram: @forgiveness_lifestyle
For bulk orders: info@forgivenesslifestyle.com

Forgiving Yourself

Forgiving Your Body Journal

Accepting the Gift of Forgiveness Journal

Forgiving People Who Reject You Journal

P.S. Forgive Yourself First Journal

Who Do You Struggle To Forgive Journal

Forgiving Your Struggle With Addiction Journal

Forgiving Your Parents

Forgiving Your Mother Journal

Forgiving Your Father Journal

Forgiving Your Parents Journal

Parenthood

Forgiving and Overcoming Mom Guilt Journal

Forgiveness Journal for Fathers

Parents Forgiving Tweens/Teen Journal

Parents Forgiving Adult Children Journal

Family

Forgiving Dead Loved One's Journal

Forgiving Family Secrets Journal

Forgiving The Bullies In Your Family Journal

Forgiving Your Siblings Journal

Marriage

Forgiving Your Wife Journal
Forgiving Your Husband Journal
Forgiving Your Mother-
In-Law Journal

Romantic Relationships

Forgiving Your Ex Journal
Forgiving The "New"
Woman Journal

Teens & Millennials

Forgiveness Journals for Teens
Forgiveness Journal
for Millennials

Religion

Forgiving God Journal
Forgiving Church People Journal

Blended Family

Forgiving A Co-Parent Journal
Forgiveness Journal
for Stepmothers
Forgiving Your
Stepmother Journal
Forgiving Your Stepkids
Mom Journal

Relationships

Forgiving Your Abuser Journal
Forgiving Friends Journal

Business/Finances

Forgiveness In Business Journal
Forgiving People At
Work Journal
Forgiving Past Money
Mistakes Journal

Sending you loving energy as you
forgive, heal, and grow.
www.forgivenesslifestyle.com

Thank You

Gratitude is the thread that weaves connections, and at this moment, I extend my most profound appreciation to those whose unwavering support and love have been the foundation of this 35-journal writing journey and beyond.

To my beloved husband, your unwavering confidence and support during our marriage and this writing project have been my anchor. Thank you for your belief in me. It has been a constant source of inspiration. Your love and presence in my life make my soul smile.

Your honesty and vulnerability to my mother led to this beautiful healing journey. Your transparency has supported my healing and given me the strength to support others on their transformational journey. I will forever be grateful for your courage to tell the truth.

My dear daughter, Shantia Dajah, your reminder to give myself grace has been a guiding light. Your wisdom transcends your years. You make my heart smile.

To my incredible son, Damien, your encouragement and motivation have fueled my determination to embark on this transformative journey. Your presence in my life is a source of boundless joy.

To Ike, my dynamic youngest son, your cheering from the sidelines has been a source of motivation and warmth. Your enthusiasm lights up my days.

My sister, Tanniedra, your unwavering belief in me and our brainstorming sessions have been invaluable. You are truly a gift.

Little sister, Jazmin, your willingness to share your experiences and vulnerability has touched my heart deeply. Your courage is inspiring.

To my "business bestie," Martha Banks Hall, the Creator of Vision Words, your prayers, encouraging texts, and our deep explorations of thoughts have been a source of clarity and growth to help me birth this project.

Denise, my beautiful friend, "The Fertility Godmother," your enthusiastic voice memos have made me feel like a rock star. Your presence has been a pillar of my strength.

To Thuy, I'm deeply grateful for your accountability and sisterhood, and I hold you as the beautiful gift you are close to my heart.

To Georgette and Cristal, your cheers have lifted my spirits. Your presence in my life is a blessing.

You all hold a special place in my heart, and I thank you from the depths of my soul for being a part of my journey.

Made in the USA
Middletown, DE
15 October 2023

40779135R00117